write if you get work
THE BEST OF BOB & RAY

BOB ELLIOTT & RAY GOULDING

...

foreword by
kurt vonnegut, jr.

write if you get work

THE BEST OF BOB & RAY

RANDOM HOUSE
NEW YORK

Library of Congress Cataloging in Publication Data

Elliott, Bob—
Write if you get work.

1. American wit and humor.   I.   Goulding, Ray,
joint author.   II.   Title.
PN6162.E45   818'.5'407   75-10297

ISBN 0-394-73244-8

Manufactured in the United States of America
24689753

*Grateful acknowledgment is made to the following for
permission to reprint text and illustrations:*

Mort Drucker: For two illustrations which appear on the title
page and the cast of characters page.

Martha Swope: For three photographs which
appear on pages 5, 29, and 125.

National Broadcasting Company, Inc.: For six photographs
which appear on pages 48, 53, 82, 96, 133, and 160.

The New Yorker: For a drawing by Thomas B. Allen which
appears on page 179. Copyright © 1973 by
The New Yorker Magazine, Inc.

Piel Bros.: For a picture of Bert and Harry. Copyright
© 1956 by Piel Bros. For a Bert and Harry
TV commercial, which appears on pages 68–69.

Newsday, Inc.: For a review by Barbara Rader
which appeared in *Newsday* on January 3, 1975, entitled
"House of Toast." Copyright © 1975 by Newsday, Inc.

Grateful acknowledgements to Herb Galewitz and Tom Koch

foreword

...

by
kurt vonnegut, jr.

It is the truth: Comedians and jazz musicians have
been more comforting and enlightening to me than
preachers or politicians or philosophers or poets or
painters or novelists of my time. Historians in the future,
in my opinion, will congratulate us on very little other
than our clowning and our jazz.

And if they know what they are doing, they will have
especially respectful words for Bob and Ray, whose book
this is. They will say, among other things, that Bob and
Ray's jokes were remarkably literary, being fun to read

...

as well as to hear. They may note, too, that Bob and Ray had such energy and such a following that they continued to create marvelous material for radio at a time when radio creatively was otherwise dead.

I have listened to Bob and Ray for years and years now—in New England, in New York City. We are about the same age, which means that we were inspired by roughly the same saints—Jack Benny, Fred Allen, W. C. Fields, Stoopnagle and Bud, and on and on. And my collected works would fill Oliver Hardy's derby, whereas theirs would fill the Astrodome.

This book contains about one ten-thousandth of their output, I would imagine. And it might be exciting to say that it represents the cream of the cream of the cream of their jokes. But the truth is that there has been an amazing evenness to their performances. I recall a single broadcast of ten years ago, for example, which might have made a book nearly as pleasant as this one.

I was in the studio when I heard it—and saw it, too. I was supposedly applying for a job as a writer for Bob and Ray. We meant to talk about the job in between comedy bits, when the microphones were dead. One of the bits, I remember, was about selling advertising space on the sides of the Bob and Ray Satellite, which was going to be orbited only twenty-eight feet off the ground.

There was an announcement, too, about the Bob and Ray Overstocked Surplus Warehouse, which was crammed with sweaters emblazoned with the letter "O." If your name didn't begin with "O," they said, they could have it legally changed for you.

And so on.

There was an episode from Mary Backstayge. Mary's actor husband, Harry, was trying to get a part in a play. His big talent, according to his supporters, was that he was wonderful at memorizing things.

There was an animal imitator who said that a pig

■ ■ ■

went "oink oink," and a cow went "moo," and that a rooster went "cock-a-doodle-doo."

I very nearly popped a gut. I am pathetically vulnerable to jokes such as these. I expect to be killed by laughter sooner or later. And I told Bob and Ray that I could never write anything as funny as what I had heard on what was for them a perfectly ordinary day.

I was puzzled that day by Bob's and Ray's melancholy. It seemed to me that they should be the happiest people on earth, but looks of sleepy ruefulness crossed their faces like clouds from time to time. I have seen those same clouds at subsequent encounters—and only now do I have a theory to explain them:

I surmise that Bob and Ray feel accursed sometimes—like crewmen on the *Flying Dutchman* or caged squirrels on an exercise wheel. They are so twangingly attuned to their era and to each other that they can go on being extremely funny almost indefinitely.

Such an unlimited opportunity to make people happy must become profoundly pooping by and by.

It occurs to me, too, as I look through this marvelous book, that Bob and Ray's jokes are singularly burglar-proof. They aren't like most other comedians' jokes these days, aren't rooted in show business and the world of celebrities and news of the day. They feature Americans who are almost fourth-rate or below, engaged in enterprises which, if not contemptible, are at least insane.

And while other comedians show us persons tormented by bad luck and enemies and so on, Bob and Ray's characters threaten to wreck themselves and their surroundings with their own stupidity. There is a refreshing and beautiful innocence in Bob's and Ray's humor.

Man is not evil, they seem to say. He is simply too hilariously stupid to survive.

And this I believe.

Cheers.

■ ■ ■

contents

■ ■ ■

Foreword by Kurt Vonnegut, Jr.   v

Wally Ballou and the Cranberry Grower   *3*
The Gathering Dusk   *7*
Prodigy Street   *10*
Elmer W. Litzinger, Spy   *14*
Editorial Reply   *17*
Audience Interview   *22*
Chocolate Wobblies   *24*
The Presidential Impersonator   *27*
Biff Burns Interviews Stuffy Hodgson   *33*
Wing Po   *37*

■ ■ ■

WADS Recruiting Announcement   *41*
Mr. Treet, Chaser of Lost People   *44*
Lawrence Fechtenberger, Interstellar Officer Candidate   *52*
Hard-Luck Stories   *56*
Mary McGoon's Recipe for Frozen Ginger Ale Salad   *60*
Squad Car 119   *62*
Lucky Phone Call   *69*
Lumber Dealers' Award   *72*
Mr. Science   *76*
The Piel Brothers: Bert's Offenses   *80*
Anxiety   *82*
Sun-Drenched Acres   *86*
Blimmix   *90*
Wally Ballou at the Sewing Contest   *94*
Mary Backstayge, Noble Wife #1   *98*
Impress-the-Boss Kit   *103*
The Orderlies   *106*
Tippy, the Wonder Dog   *110*
Mary Backstayge, Noble Wife #2   *114*
Oatmeal for Thanksgiving   *121*
Webley L. Webster: Wisdom of the Ages   *124*
Cadenza   *127*
Spelling Bee   *131*
State Your Case   *140*
Charley Chipmunk Club   *144*
Children's Menu   *148*
Food and Drink Imitator   *151*
The Defenseless   *154*
Money-Saving Tips   *158*
Emergency Ward   *160*
Light Bulb Collector   *164*
Barry Campbell   *168*
The Pittmans   *173*
The Do-It-Yourselfer   *179*
Travelogue   *183*
Bridget Hillary and the News   *187*
Person-of-the-Month Club   *191*
Bob and Ray Reunite the Whirleys   *195*
Widen Your Horizons   *199*
Rorshack   *203*
Preston Turnbridge, Lighthouse Keeper   *207*

■ ■ ■

featuring

Wally Ballou   Pop Beloved   Mary McGoon
   Edna Bessinger   Mr. Science   Mary Backstayge
         Webley L. Webster   Barry Campbell
Calvin Hoogevin   Biff Burns
         Wally, the Word Man   Elmer W. Litzinger, Spy
   Rorshack   Tippy, the Wonder Dog   Mr. Wise Old Owl
Word Carr   Arch Rolandson   Stuffy Hodgson   Wing Po
         Commissioner Herman Schlepheimer
   Mr. Treet, Chaser of Lost People   Greg Marlowe
Joe Blimmix   Messmore Tisdale   Mug Mellish
   Wealthy Jacobus Pike   Wanda Stapp   Clifton Nefty
Nola Krowdish Bosworth Hartley Ralph R. Kruger, Junior
                  G. E. Porgy   Ramses Fletch
   Lawrence Fechtenberger, Interstellar Officer Candidate
         Jimmy Schwab   Commander Neville Putney
Chief Orderly Schnellwell   Grandpa Witherspoon
   Jimmy Joe Pittman   Captain Parker Gibbes
         Stock Vanderhoogen   Benjamin Franklin
Illegal Left Turn Bronson   Itchy Rainbolt
   Fentriss Synom   Attorney Millard Shifton   Fred Falvy
Doctor Gerhart Snutton   Augustus Winesap
Bridget Hillary   Preston Turnbridge

...

write if
you get work
THE BEST OF
BOB & RAY

bulletin

...

*From the Office of Fluctuation Control,
Bureau of Edible Condiments; Soluble,
Insoluble, and Indigestible Fats and
Glutinous Derivatives, Washington, D.C.:
Directive 943456201: As of September
1st, the price of groundhog meat will be
fixed at a level no higher than the price
of groundhog meat on October 15, 1974.*

wally ballou
and the
cranberry grower

■ ■ ■

From Bob and Ray: The Two and Only

BOB   Good day, folks, this is Bob Elliott . . .

RAY   . . . And Ray Goulding. We've just had word from correspondent Wally Ballou that there's a fast-breaking news story not far from here. So, in Times Square, come in, please, Wally Ballou.

BALLOU   . . . ly Ballou in Times Square. I've discovered that some of my best stories come from merely striking up a conversation with the man in the street . . . and this gentleman looks as if he might have

■ ■ ■

such a story. Could I have your name, sir, and what you do?

SMITH   Ward Smith . . . I'm a cranberry grower. I own cranberry bogs.

BALLOU   Very interesting. I've always been curious to know a little bit about the raising of cranberries. They're such beautiful things when you see them growing. You have to be very careful of frosts, don't you?

SMITH   That's right. You have to flood the bogs if there's a danger of frost. And then you harvest them when they're big and red and ripe and juicy and bitter as anything!

BALLOU   Wally Ballou here in Times Square with a fast-breaking cranberry story, ladies and gentlemen! After you harvest them, Mr. Smith, do you have your own processing plant?

SMITH   Processing plant? What do you mean by that, Mr. Ballou?

BALLOU   By that, I mean, do you have your own factory for squeezing the juice out of the cranberries?

SMITH   Squeezing the juice out of cranberries? I never heard of—

BALLOU   Yes . . . to make cranberry juice.

SMITH   *Juice*? Out of cranberries?

BALLOU   Yes, for your cranberry juice cocktails.

SMITH   Cranberry juice cocktails?

BALLOU   Or perhaps you make cranberry sauce out of them?

SMITH   What would that be for? A dessert?

■ ■ ■

BALLOU   No, you serve it as a side dish . . . with turkey or meats.

SMITH   Well, I never! You know, you've triggered something here.

BALLOU   Then you can make sherbet out of them. That's especially good after a big meal. Very refreshing.

SMITH   Say, have you got a pencil? I want to write all this down.

BALLOU   Sure . . . here.

SMITH   Now, let's see . . . Can you make glass out of them?

BALLOU   No, you can't make glass out of them!

SMITH   Give it all to me again. (*He begins to write*)

BALLOU   Okay. Well, there's cranberry juice.

SMITH   J–U—How do you spell that?

BALLOU   I–C–E.

SMITH   What?

BALLOU   I–C–E.

SMITH   I–C–E . . . I thought there was a "J" in juice.

BALLOU   J–U–I–C–E!

SMITH   Oh, yes.

BALLOU   Cranberry sauce.

SMITH   Sauce . . .

BALLOU   There's also cranberry jelly. That's delicious too.

SMITH   What would that have—pectin in it or something?

■ ■ ■

BALLOU   I don't know what's in it, but it's good.

SMITH   Well, thank you very much, Mr. Ballou. You've sure opened my eyes to some of the uses for cranberries.

BALLOU   Before you go, Mr. Smith, can I ask you one question?

SMITH   *Sure*.

BALLOU   All of these years that you've been growing cranberries . . . What have you been doing with them?

SMITH   I've been selling them in a basket, like strawberries. For cranberry shortcake. And do you know . . . they really don't sell that way?

BALLOU   I should imagine not. Thanks, Mr. Smith . . . and now, this is broadcasting's silver-throated Wally Ballou returning it to the studio . . .

■ ■ ■

the
gathering
dusk

. . .

(Theme music)

ANNOUNCER   And now the makers of Grime, the magic
shortening that spreads like lard, invite you to join
us for another episode of *The Gathering Dusk*.
(Music up and under) As we look in on the Bessinger household today, Edna is still bedridden. It
is later afternoon, and Dr. Harper is just entering
the room . . .

(Sound: Door shutting)

. . .

EDNA Doctor, I've been bedridden for a good number of years, now, and I think it's time for you to be telling me the truth.

DOCTOR I'm telling you the truth, Edna. There isn't a thing in the world wrong with you. You're as sound as a dollar.

EDNA I've always had hammer toes, Doctor, you know that.

DOCTOR Hammer toes are no reason for staying in bed, Edna. I haven't seen you downtown in Red Boiling Springs since the fall of '67.

EDNA It was the spring of '66, Dr. Harper.

DOCTOR I think it was the fall of '67, Edna.

EDNA Spring of '66.

DOCTOR Well, anyway . . . why don't you leave the house? It'd do you a world of good.

EDNA I can't leave the house if I'm bedridden, doctor. The bed won't go through the door.

DOCTOR Well, get out of bed. There's nothing wrong with you. Why should you stay in bed? You're afraid you'll meet David down in the village, aren't you?

EDNA Yes, I am. I just don't know what I'd do if I saw him face to face again.

DOCTOR But David's been missing for ten years now. He couldn't still be in town. Somebody would have seen him.

EDNA He's hiding in the loft of Grimsley's barn. That's where he is. He used to tell me that someday he was going to chuck it all . . . and go up in the loft of Grimsley's barn and stay there. That's what he's done, I just know it.

■ ■ ■

8

DOCTOR   Well, suppose he is up there? Suppose you met him in the village? What could happen? You keep saying it's all over between you two, anyway.

EDNA   It's the children, Doctor. I've got to think of them, don't I?

DOCTOR   Edna, you don't have any children.

EDNA   Of course I do. Patty and David, Junior.

DOCTOR   Those aren't your children. They belong to the Fergusons down the street. They come into the yard, here, to play once in a while.

EDNA   I just assumed that they were mine. I remember David always used to say he was going to leave the children to me and go live in the loft of Grimsley's barn.

DOCTOR   Well, David was a looney, Edna, we both know that.

EDNA   Doctor, I can't tell you what this news means to me. It's as if a great weight had been lifted from my shoulders . . . and I'm no longer standing in . . . the Gathering Dusk.

(Theme music in and under)

ANNOUNCER   Ladies, no one likes a shortening filled with lumps and foreign objects. That's why you'll like Grime, the magic shortening that spreads like lard. Try some today. And be sure to join us next time, when Edna goes to the village . . . in *The Gathering Dusk*.

(Music up and out)

■ ■ ■

prodigy street

■ ■ ■

(Bouncy type of theme music. Establish and fade for)

WALLY   Hi there, boys and girls. Let's all gather round
for another session of fun and learning on . . .
Prodigy Street. I know how anxious all you little
people are to become smarter than your mommies
and daddies. So let's not waste another minute to
find out what Mr. Wise Old Owl has to teach us
today. I see you have your blackboard all set up
there ready to begin, Mr. Owl.

■ ■ ■

OWL   Yes, I sure do, Wally the Word Man. And today, boys and girls, we're going to learn a lot more about numbers as we study the numeral 1. First, I'm going to put a figure 1 on my Wise Old Owl blackboard. And to help you remember, we'll write out the word "one" right next to it—O–N–E. Now, we'll put—

WALLY   Excuse me, Mr. Wise Old Owl. But I think the boys and girls should notice that the word "one" begins with that "W" sound I was telling them about yesterday on *Prodigy Street*. But it isn't spelled with a "W." How about that?!

OWL   Well, that's certainly interesting, Wally the Word Man. But today's lesson is about numbers. So I want all of you boys and girls to hold up one finger and then count it.

WALLY   But first, kids, you should take a moment to notice that "one" is spelled as if it should be pronounced "own." But always remember—it isn't.

OWL   Pardon me, Wally the Word Man. But I don't think we should confuse the boys and girls with too many ideas at once here. And I'd just asked them to count a finger when I'm afraid you got them off onto something else.

WALLY   I'm terribly sorry, Mr. Wise Old Owl. It's just that we were learning about the letter "W" yesterday. And I thought it would be good to bring up this point while it was fresh in mind. But that was all. So please continue.

OWL   Thank you . . . Now, kids, hold up one more finger and count again. How many are there this time? That's right—two. So one plus one makes two. Now I'll put the figure 2 on the blackboard—and right next to it, the word "two"—T–W–O.

■ ■ ■

WALLY   Well, look there, boys and girls. Our old friend, the letter "W," is peeking out at us from the middle of the word "two."

OWL   Look, Wally—I really wish you'd knock it off with this letter "W" business. I'm trying to teach the kids simple addition.

WALLY   Well, actually, that's not a very important thing to know. But the word "two" is unique in our language. See, kids? It's spelled as if it should be pronounced "twah." But always remember—it isn't.

OWL   Wally, nobody needs to know how it's spelled to do arithmetic. For all I know, Einstein couldn't spell it.

WALLY   Well, I don't think our producer is going to be too happy to hear you implying to the boys and girls that Einstein was illiterate.

OWL   I didn't say that. I just mean it's completely beside the point. You don't have to be able to spell numbers to do arithmetic. It's irrelevant . . . Now hold up another finger, kids, and—

WALLY   Well, I certainly don't consider any phase of the correct use of our language to be irrelevant. And I think you may be right out on your ear when the foundation that finances this show hears what you said.

OWL   Why do you have to twist around everything I say? You English grammar smart alecks are always doing that. And I've got millions of kids out there holding up three fingers waiting for me to tell them what to do next.

WALLY   Well, I suppose you're just going to have them count their fingers again. So count your fingers, kids . . . Big deal!

■ ■ ■

OWL Now, just hold on. Are you trying to make me look foolish in front of all these children?

WALLY I sure don't have to try very hard to do that, fella.

OWL Okay, Buster. If you're looking for a knuckle sandwich, you got one. Take that!

(*Sound: Scuffling, furniture and glass breaking, Wally and Owl grunting and groaning. Then*)

WALLY (*Breathless*) Time's up for today's lesson, kids. But join us again tomorrow on *Prodigy Street* for more—

OWL (*Breathless*) You can stop holding your fingers up in the air now, boys and girls.

(*Bring in theme music during*)

WALLY Yeah, stop that. But remember to tune in tomorrow for more fun and learning—same time, same station—on *Prodigy Street*. See you then, Mr. Wise Old Owl.

OWL Yeah. I suppose so.

(*Theme music up briefly and then out*)

■ ■ ■

elmer w. litzinger, spy

. . .

(Dramatic theme music. Establish and under for)

ANNOUNCER   And now the makers of Tingle—the long-wearing dental floss created from spun glass fiber—invite you to join us for another exciting adventure of *Elmer W. Litzinger, Spy.*

(Theme music up briefly and then out)

LITZINGER   My name is Elmer W. Litzinger, Spy. I work with quiet efficiency on some of the toughest

. . .

espionage assignments our government can hand out. Recently, we got word that a hostile foreign power was trying to crack the secret code that our Navy uses in the Pacific. It was my job to find out if the enemy had been successful. So I went to an island near the Philippines where foreign ships re-fuel—and made my way to a tavern that I knew was a favorite hangout for visiting sailors . . .

(Sound: General crowd noise under and hold for)

BARTENDER   What'll it be, Mac? Beer?

LITZINGER   A blue moon over salmon-pink mountains.

BARTENDER   Sorry. I don't know much about making those fancy cocktails. What's in it?

LITZINGER   Oh, that's not a drink, my good man. I thought you were one of our agents, so I gave you the secret greeting. You see, I'm Elmer W. Litzinger, Spy. Here's my business card.

BARTENDER   That's very interesting. I never saw a business card laid out this way—with the phone number in the middle. Thirteen—ten—twenty-one—

LITZINGER   Oh, that's not my phone number. That's my name printed in the secret code our Navy uses here in the Pacific. I had those cards made up as sort of a gag to hand out to my fellow agents. They appreciate a good laugh.

BARTENDER   Oh, me, too. Of course, I don't get the full benefit of the joke because I don't know the code. But I assume the thirteen is the first letter in your name, and ten is the second, and like that.

LITZINGER   Yes. It's really quite simple. You just number the letters of the alphabet from one to twenty-six—and then add 1 to each number so it becomes a code that's impossible to crack.

■ ■ ■

BARTENDER   Oh, I get it. Your name's Litzinger. And "L" is the twelfth letter in the alphabet. But you add one to make it thirteen. And then the letter "I" is—

LITZINGER   Well, you don't need to work out the whole thing. It's just a dull job once you know how the code operates.

BARTENDER   Gee, I don't think it's dull. I like working puzzles. In fact, my employer gives prizes to us for figuring out things like this.

LITZINGER   Really? Is the contest open to anyone?

BARTENDER   No, I don't think you could enter. You see, the answers all have to be put on microfilm and then sent to a secret address in the capital city of a hostile country.

LITZINGER   Hmm. That's a rather complicated way to run a prize contest. It's almost like our espionage operation.

BARTENDER   Yeah. It's almost like ours, too . . . Incidentally, what's this number I here on the card in the middle of your name?

LITZINGER   Oh, that's the "Z" in Litzinger. You see, "Z" is the last letter in the alphabet. So when you add one to it, that puts you back at the beginning again.

BARTENDER   Hey, that's clever. It might have taken me several minutes to figure that out if you hadn't told me.

LITZINGER   Well, of course, after you'd gotten all the other letters in my name, you'd have known that the middle one had to be a "Z."

BARTENDER   Yeah. That's the way I would have figured

■ ■ ■

it out all right. But as I say, it might have taken several minutes. And I want to hurry and get this microfilmed so I can ship it out on the last submarine leaving tonight.

LITZINGER   That's strange. I didn't see any submarines anchored in the harbor.

BARTENDER   Oh, well, you wouldn't have seen this one. It's right underneath one of your battleships.

LITZINGER   I see. And I suppose the sailors in here with funny lettering on their caps are the crewmen.

BARTENDER   Yeah, all but one of them. He's assigned to keep an eye on you.

LITZINGER   Really? I suspected there might be a spy in here somewhere—and you've just enabled me to identify him as one of those forty sailors. I'm sure when I file my daily report, this will bring me a commendation from the home office, saying: "Foreign agent cleverly spotted by Elmer W. Litzinger, Spy."

(Theme music. Establish and under for)

ANNOUNCER   Friends, we know how much you've enjoyed this fine dramatic program. So why not show your appreciation by stocking up now on our sponsor's fine product—Tingle. And join us soon for more exciting adventures in the career of . . . Elmer W. Litzinger, Spy.

(Theme music up briefly and then out)

■ ■ ■

editorial
reply

. . .

BOB   As you may remember, we presented a Bob and
Ray editorial recently in which we gave our thought-
ful reasons for opposing the reelection of Hubert C.
Murdock to the city council of Patchford, Connecti-
cut. We recognize our responsibility to present
opposing viewpoints. So here to respond to that
Bob and Ray editorial is the honorable Hubert C.
Murdock—alderman from the fourth district of
Patchford, Connecticut.

MURDOCK   Thank you. My dear friends and fellow citi-

. . .

zens of Patchford. I have been the victim of a vicious attack by—

BOB Excuse me just a moment, Alderman. I forgot to mention one thing. For the benefit of our listening audience, Mr. Murdock is appearing today in accordance with the equal time provision of the Federal Communications Code. The opinions he expresses are solely his own and do not necessarily reflect the viewpoint of this station. Very well, Mr. Murdock. You may continue now.

MURDOCK Well, you really let the air out of my balloon with that comment, fella. What are you trying to do—say I'm a liar before I even open my mouth?

BOB No, not at all, sir. That's just a disclaimer that our legal department requires us to read. After all, we don't know what you plan to say.

MURDOCK So you just assume it's going to be a pack of lies. Is that it?

BOB No. We don't assume anything. It's just a standard formality. Now, please, try not to take umbrage, and just go ahead and read your statement.

MURDOCK Well, for your information, I've already taken umbrage. But you can't shut me up. I'm going to read this statement anyway.

BOB Well, I wish you would. So please begin.

MURDOCK I fully intend to . . . My dear friends and fellow citizens of Patchford. I have been the victim of a vicious attack by the Bob and Ray organization. Their recent editorial has opposed my bid for reelection without giving valid reasons for that opposition. However, I know full well— Aw, now, wait a minute. What are you doing over there, pal— snickering behind my back?

■ ■ ■

19

BOB   No. I'm not doing anything. I was just trimming this hangnail while I wait for you to finish.

MURDOCK   Yeah? Well, I've been watching you out of the corner of my eye—and I saw you smirk.

BOB   I wasn't smirking, Alderman. I was just squinting to see if I got this nail even with the others. Now, please continue.

MURDOCK   Okay. But just don't let me catch you doing it again . . . My fellow citizens, I know the real reason—the unspoken reason—why Bob and Ray are trying to end my illustrious career. But let me say that what they're thinking is based entirely on irresponsible gossip. I am not even acquainted with a cocktail waitress named Lou Ann. And I was nowhere near the vicinity of Pittsfield, Massachusetts, on the night of September 23.

BOB   Excuse me, Alderman. But are you sure you want to be saying things like this in reply to our editorial?

MURDOCK   You shut up and go trim your fingernails some more.

BOB   Well, it's just that we didn't mention anything about—

MURDOCK   Never mind what you mentioned. I know what you were thinking. But there's not a shred of evidence to support the charge. And that goes for my alleged behavior at last summer's conference on civic government, too. As my constituents know, that meeting was held in Las Vegas—where many temptations are placed in the path of an honest man. But the rumors that have circulated are groundless. Even if I had wanted to do what people are saying, I couldn't have done it because the betting limit at the blackjack table is five hundred

■ ■ ■

dollars. And so—having cleared my good name—I thank you.

BOB   You have been listening to a reply to a Bob and Ray editorial. Our speaker today has been—

MURDOCK   Please! Now that I've thought about it, I wish you wouldn't mention my name again.

BOB   I understand. You did seem to get a little carried away there.

MURDOCK   Yeah. I don't know what gets into me. Once I start to prattle, I really dig a hole for myself. So just forget I was here. Goodbye.

(*Sound: Hurried footsteps and door slam*)

BOB   Today's editorial reply has been presented under the auspices of the Bob and Ray Public Affairs Department. Qualified persons wishing to reply to this reply are wholeheartedly encouraged *not* to do so.

■ ■ ■

audience
interview

. . .

BOB Let's meet some of our Bob and Ray audience and see who is from the most distant point from New York. Anyone here from a great distance away?

MAN A thousand one hundred miles away . . .

BOB And what do you call home, sir?

MAN Straight down!

BOB You live in the ground?

. . .

MAN Yes, sir.

BOB You've lived there all your life?

MAN No. Just about fifteen years ago, I dug down and liked it down there.

BOB It's cool, I suppose.

MAN It's cool, yes.

BOB Any particular advantages to living in the earth this way?

MAN Er . . . well . . . no. But then, there are the same advantages and disadvantages as you'd have if you were living, say, one thousand one hundred miles up in a tree!

BOB Of course, you can get a good laugh when you tell someone you live a thousand one hundred miles away.

MAN Straight down! It's a long walk . . . and I only have steps for nine hundred. The last two hundred miles is a slide!

■ ■ ■

chocolate wobblies

■ ■ ■

RAY Ah, there's good news today, friends.

BOB Good news for you, folks, bad news for us.

RAY We've done it again, and our loss is your gain.

BOB You see, in anticipation of the Easter season, we laid in a large supply of chocolate rabbits.

RAY These were the best chocolate rabbits money could buy. Each one was genuine chocolate, all chocolate.

■ ■ ■

24

BOB   Each one had a purple ribbon tied around his or her neck.

RAY   Each one was edible, real edible.

BOB   But, through the carelessness of one of our alert uniformed attendants, these chocolate rabbits were stored next to the steampipes in our overstocked surplus warehouse.

RAY   So, we are now able to offer, at a ridiculously low price, exactly twenty gross of genuine, laughably edible, all chocolate *wobblies.*

BOB   These wobblies are not only appropriate for any season, but the kiddies will have great fun trying to guess what the wobblies are supposed to represent.

RAY   Some of you imaginative youngsters will recognize dinosaurs, wombats and anteaters.

BOB   Others will see pterodactyls, vultures and your mother-in-law.

RAY   But, friends, this is backed up by the Bob and Ray unconditional guarantee . . . not one of the kiddies will know these were once rabbits.

BOB   Any wobblie mistaken for a wabbit can be returned to the Bob and Ray overstocked surplus warehouse, where the full purchase price will be laughingly returned.

RAY   Never again do we expect to be able to make this amazing offer.

BOB   The warehouse engineers have already removed the steampipes, and with them, our alert uniformed attendant.

RAY   So be the first in your neighborhood to surprise your kiddies after Easter! And remember, each of

■ ■ ■

these edible all-chocolate wobblies has, *somewhere in it* . . . a real purple ribbon!

BOB And that makes an extra surprise that really will give the little nippers a bang . . . Also pull out any loose teeth that they may have been trying to dislodge.

RAY So write immediately to "Windfall," New York, New York.

BOB And say, "We'll bite."

■ ■ ■

the
presidential
impersonator

■ ■ ■

RAY It isn't often that you see me here jumping in my
seat with excitement, because we have seen many
exciting things come and go. Today, however, I
believe we have topped them all . . . sitting opposite
me in the little booth is one of the greatest im-
personators that I have had the privilege to know
and to talk with. He has been here an hour and he
had us all awe-stricken as he ran through many of
his impersonations. For those listening, I wonder if
you will repeat your name?

■ ■ ■

ROLANDSON   Arch Rolandson.

RAY   Arch Rolandson. Would you care to tell the audience what you do?

ROLANDSON   I'm rather modest, so if you . . .

RAY   Mr. Rolandson here impersonates Presidents, Presidents who served before 1900, and so we are going to sit in on a little bit of history. How did you get their voices down?

ROLANDSON   First, of course, I had to study the lives of the Presidents, their personal habits, their family relationships, their part in American history.

RAY   And their famous speeches, too?

ROLANDSON   Oh, no, I lay off their speeches. I concentrated on the things that they said in everyday life . . . like going to the store.

RAY   All right, who is the first President you are going to impersonate?

ROLANDSON   Martin Van Buren!

RAY   Martin Van Buren!

ROLANDSON   He sounds something like this . . . (*No change in voice*) Would you give me three pounds of white flour, please?

RAY   That's President Van Buren when he went to the store.

ROLANDSON   Would you like to hear Jimmy Madison? Okay . . . (*No change in voice*) I say, it looks like we are going to have rain before morning.

RAY   That was former President James Madison. Who else do you do?

■ ■ ■

ROLANDSON   Practically anyone that you can mention. How about Franklin Pierce? But then I don't do him well. I think the one that I do the best is President John Polk. He sounded something like this as he walked down the street and spied a friend: "Hello, there."

RAY   That was President *James* Polk.

ROLANDSON   No, that was President *John* Polk.

RAY   I don't think we had a President *John* Polk, I know we had a *James* Polk. But, Arch, I am not jumping around in my seat now as much as I was before.

ROLANDSON   You do seem to have calmed down!

■ ■ ■

bulletin

...

Here is a supplementary bulletin from the Office of Fluctuation Control, Bureau of Edible Condiments; Soluble, Insoluble, and Indigestible Fats and Glutinous Derivatives, Washington, D.C. Correction of Directive 943456201, issued a while back, concerning the fixed price of groundhog meat. In the directive above named, the quotation on groundhog meat should read ground hogmeat.

biff burns
interviews
stuffy hodgson

■ ■ ■

From Bob and Ray: The Two and Only

BIFF   Hi, sports fans. This is Biff Burns and it's pre-game dugout dialogue time. We're going to talk to the grizzled veteran of some twenty-odd years in baseball who today is finally retiring—Stuffy Hodgson. Stuffy, how do you feel?

STUFF   Well, I'm a bit sad, Biff. After all these years in the game . . . to realize this is my last day.

BIFF   That's a normal feeling to have, Stuff . . . but

■ ■ ■

looking back, you've got to agree the game's been pretty good to you.

STUFF Not as good to me as it has been to some of these young punks coming along!

BIFF I sense a note of rancor there. What do you mean?

STUFF Well, I'll tell you . . . I think probably the game has passed me by, Biff.

BIFF Is that so?

STUFF You see, the kids coming up nowadays, all they care about is money. Now, when I signed up, it was for the love of the game. These young kids—all they think about now is money, beautiful women, making TV commercials, big cars, big homes, vintage wines, makin' movies . . . and, er—sleepin' late.

BIFF I guess guys like you went wrong somewhere along the line, huh?

STUFF Well, I don't know. You know, they have these radios, and they have all this music goin' in the locker room. I don't understand it. It's a bunch of noise. Whatever happened to Kate Smith . . . and Pat Boone . . . and them guys?

BIFF I don't know.

STUFF Now, they sang real songs! And another thing . . . these guys are always playing these jokes.

BIFF Like what?

STUFF Like the other day, they loosened my spikes so I'd run wobbly. Then they put Limburger cheese up in the sweatband of my cap. Took me half the season to track down that smell. The other day, they threw water on me and one of the sports reporters.

■ ■ ■

BIFF   Yeah, I think I read about that.

STUFF   I just don't understand the game any more.

BIFF   But despite all this I'm glad to see one thing, Stuffy. After this long career of yours, its ups and downs, you've managed to retain your sense of humor!

STUFF   You have to!

BIFF   Could you give us one of those baseball anecdotes that you tell at the sports dinners?

STIFF   Well, I remember the first day I came up to bat in the big leagues. They had this big left-hander out on the mound. You remember him?

BIFF   Sure do.

STUFF   Well, he was throwin' real smoke that day. I couldn't see a thing. So the umpire—You remember him? Great big guy behind the plate?

BIFF   I don't think I remember him, no.

STUFF   Well, when the third strike went by, he says: "You're out!" I was so mad, I took my bat and I threw it straight up in the air, see? And the umpire took off his mask, and he said to me, "Young man . . ." (I was a young man then) "young man, if that bat comes down, you're out of the game!"

BIFF   Great story, Stuffy. Just one more question, Stuff. Over the years, you've come to be known as a guy who likes to bend the old elbow a little bit. You haven't spent much time worrying about what you ate or drank, or how much. Still and all, you seem to be in pretty good shape. How do you account for that?

STUFF   Imitation turf is the worst thing that's ever hap-

■ ■ ■

35

pened to baseball. It's a little like playing on a billiard table. The ball takes crazy bounces, hops up and hits your infielders in the clavicle. Your feet don't grip into it, enabling you to make the play . . . which you've got to make if you're going to win the game. And that goes for both teams, equally!!!

BIFF   Stuffy, do you think they're going to retire your number now?

STUFF   Naw. I think one of the young punks is wearing it already!

BIFF   Well, I see the Mayor and Mickey Mantle and George Jessel coming into the dugout for your retirement ceremonies, so I'll just wish you a lot of luck, Stuffy. We'll see you around . . . And this is Biff Burns saying, until next time, this is Biff Burns saying so long.

■ ■ ■

wing po

■ ■ ■

(Oriental music. Establish and under for)

ANNOUNCER Welcome now to another episode of *Wing Po*—the true-to-life story of a Chinese philosopher who wanders across the American frontier in search of work. As our action-packed drama begins today, Wing Po has just entered the small, run-down saloon at Bitter Creek, and is approaching the bar.

(Sound: Footsteps)

BARTENDER Howdy there, young fella. What'll it be?

■ ■ ■

PO   (*Slow, thoughtful and slightly Chinese throughout*) It will be as it has always been—for life is much like the rolling wheel of the oxcart. If we are to know how the spokes shall move on the next turn, we need only remember what they have done before.

BARTENDER   Oh. You're from out of town, ain't you?

PO   The thought you express reflects knowledge. I have traveled far in the hope that I may see from below the same tree limbs which the soaring hawk can only see from above.

BARTENDER   Uh-huh. Do you want to give me your drink order now—or do you think maybe you've already had too much?

PO   I do not seek the goods you sell, for the drink that deadens the mind must also blur the inward vision of the spirit. And he who sees only outward is much like the snowflake which can fall no other way except down.

BARTENDER   Look, fella, I don't want to seem unfriendly, but why are you taking up space at my bar if you ain't planning to be a customer?

PO   I intend to be no more burden upon you than the meadowlark who rides the buffalo. I am here in search of honest work.

BARTENDER   Well, why didn't you say so? I take on drifters here from time to time. What can you do? Tend bar? Deal faro?

PO   I can offer the philosophy that opens the gate to age-old wisdom.

BARTENDER   Yeah. Well, everybody who comes in here thinks he can do that. All I need is somebody to wash beer glasses for fifty cents a day and meals.

■ ■ ■

PO   Your generosity overwhelms. But the rainbow of color left by nature upon the dirty glass is not a thing to be washed away. It must first be held to the light and carefully perceived.

BARTENDER   Well, if you're fixing to perceive every glass before you wash it, I couldn't go any higher than two bits a day.

PO   So it shall be. And I will also play my flute for your dancing girls to shuffle their feet to.

(*Sound: Approaching footsteps*)

BARTENDER'S WIFE   (*Falsetto*) Clifford, why are you standing here talking to the only customer in the place when there's booze to be toted from the cellar?

PO   Please! Do not place the blame upon his shoulders. The fault for speaking too long is mine—but I find it difficult to dispense only a little wisdom.

BARTENDER'S WIFE   Clifford, who is this clown in the kimono staring through the empty beer glass?

PO   I am Wing Po and—

BARTENDER   He's a philosopher I hired to wash the glassware, Nettie. But right now, he's just perceiving that empty one first.

PO   It is true, for—

BARTENDER'S WIFE   He's doing what with it?

PO   It is sometimes a hard thing to explain.

BARTENDER   No, it ain't. He's perceiving the beer glass, Nettie. He says nature puts all kinds of rainbows and things inside dirty beer glasses. So he's got to perceive each one before he washes it.

PO   He speaks the truth. See how the yellows and golds

■ ■ ■

39

catch the glimmerings of light? For one who seeks to know the ingredients of the sunrise—look no further.

BARTENDER'S WIFE Well, we've had a lot of loonies around this place. But you're the first one who thought the sunrise was made out of stale beer. Now, are you going to pick up your flute and leave or shall I part your hair with this crowbar?

PO Let there be no violence. I shall go, for destiny has so ordered it. Bye-bye.

(*Theme music. Establish and under for*)

ANNOUNCER And so, our hero moves on to his next exciting adventure. Be sure to join us soon for more action-packed drama in the thrilling life of . . . *Wing Po*.

(*Theme music up and then out*)

■ ■ ■

WADS
recruiting
announcement

. . .

BOB Ladies, here's your chance to have clean, whole-some adventure, while serving your municipality.

RAY You can earn good pay, too, by enlisting now in WADS—the Women's Auxiliary of the Department of Sanitation.

BOB The Department of Sanitation needs women to work side by side with the men on the street.

RAY Experience the thrill of riding the big General

. . .

Grant sanitation trucks side by side with the city's crack garbage collectors.

BOB See strange parts of town. Travel new streets and avenues, new highways and byways.

RAY If you enlist now, you can have your choice of any branch of the service—garbage, ashes or regular trash.

BOB Listen to what Sanitation Commissioner Herman Schlepheimer has to say about the WADS.

SCHLEP Say, girls, you don't know the fun you're missing by not joining the Women's Auxiliary of the Department of Sanitation. The WADS is not all work and no play. No, ma'am. There are jolly weekly get-togethers in the department canteen where you will meet handsome clean-cut sanitation men. You will enjoy the swap sessions, when collectors from every route exchange items they have salvaged during the day's campaign.

BOB Mr. Schlepheimer, isn't it true also that the ladies will wear the smartest of uniforms?

SCHLEP I'm glad you mentioned that, Bob. Yes, it's true. The WADS uniform is one of the slinkiest of any city service. It was especially designed by the great French couturier, Mme. Scallopine.

BOB What about promotions?

SCHLEP I'm glad you mentioned that, Bob. Promotions are frequent in the WADS. The new recruit, of course, starts as a kicker.

BOB What is that, sir?

SCHLEP Well, she will be assigned to work with a non-commissioned can heaver. When the noncom heaves a can of garbage into the truck, some bits and pieces

■ ■ ■

naturally fall to the ground. The recruit's job is to kick those bits and pieces around till they get lost.

BOB   And what's the next step up the line of promotion?

SCHLEP   That would be the job of can selector. In this job the lady walks ahead of the truck and chooses which cans will be emptied and which cans will be ignored.

BOB   I suppose there's no limit to the rank which a lady can achieve.

SCHLEP   No, Bob, there isn't. A loyal, hard-working WAD can eventually rise to a choice spot on the Dawn Patrol.

BOB   What would she do then?

SCHLEP   She'd have the much-envied job of banging empty garbage cans while the city sleeps.

BOB   Thank you, Mr. Schlepheimer, for telling us about the Women's Auxiliary of the Department of Sanitation, whose slogan is "We have just WADS of fun!"

■ ■ ■

mr. treet, chaser of lost people

...

(Music: Somber and mysterious)

BOB It's mystery time on the Bob and Ray show. Presenting Mr. Treet, Chaser of Lost People. Today, the surly old investigator takes from his files the case he calls, "The Overdose of Very Fatal Poison Murder Clue."

(Music: Out)

BOB Our story opens in the luxurious New York penthouse apartment of Wealthy Jacobus Pike, famous

...

backer of Broadway plays. As we hear Pike call for his valet, Rudy . . .

PIKE   Rudy, come here!

(*Door opens*)

RUDY   (*Coming on*) You call, Mr. Pike?

PIKE   Yes, Rudy. I want you to take this manuscript back to Greg Marlowe, young playwright who is secretly in love with my sister, Julia, who dreams of a career on the stage. There is a note inside which explains to him my reason for refusing to back his play on Broadway.

RUDY   Okay, Mr. Pike. I'll be back as soon as possible.

(*Door closes*)

PIKE   That young upstart thinks he can coerce me into putting up my money for any such ridiculous play as that. Well, he has another— What? How did you get in here? What do you want? No, no, don't shoot me with that gun you're holding. I'll do anything. Don't come any closer. No, no.

(*Gunshots; body falls to floor*)

PIKE   Oooh. You've murdered me. You sneaked in here wearing the disguise of someone I don't know, waited until I was alone and then you killed me. (*Moaning*) I'm dead.

BOB   Several hours later in the office of Mr. Treet, Chaser of Lost People, we see the surly old investigator at his desk as his assistant Spike Glancy ushers in a tall young man with dark features. We hear Spike say . . .

SPIKE   This gentleman wants to see you, boss.

TREET   Usher him in, Spike.

■ ■ ■

SPIKE   He's a tall young man with dark features.

TREET   I can see that, Spike.

SPIKE   He looks guilty to me, boss.

TREET   No man is innocent if he is proven guilty, Spike. Show him in.

SPIKE   You see, mister? I told you Mr. Treet was fair.

TREET   That will be all, Spike. Sit down, sir.

SPIKE   I'll be right outside if you need me, boss.

TREET   All right.

(*Door closes*)

TREET   Now, what can I do for you, sir?

MARLOWE   Mr. Treet, I am Gregory Marlowe, young playwright secretly in love with Wealthy Jacobus Pike's sister, Julia, who dreams of a career on the stage.

TREET   (*Interrupting*) Come, come, young man, you'll have to put your cards on the table if you want me to help you.

MARLOWE   I'm coming to that, Mr. Treet. This morning I went to Pike's expensive New York penthouse apartment . . .

TREET   (*Interrupting*) You went there believing that Pike's sister, Julia, had talked her brother, Wealthy Jacobus, into putting up the money for the new play that you've written.

MARLOWE   Mr. Treet, you're uncanny!

TREET   I'm right, then?

MARLOWE   No. I went there expecting to have Pike

■ ■ ■

46

give me a check for my play so that I can start producing it next week.

TREET   Aha! What did you find, Marlowe?

MARLOWE   I found Pike dead, Mr. Treet.

TREET   Dead?

MARLOWE   Dead, Mr. Treet. Murdered by an overdose of a very fatal poison.

TREET   Dreadful! And you want me . . .?

MARLOWE   I want you to help me, Mr. Treet.

TREET   Well, I'll do my best. My assistant Spike and you and I will first go to the murdered man's apartment. Oh, Spike?

SPIKE   Yes, boss?

TREET   Open the door before you come in.

SPIKE   Oh, I'm sorry.

(*Door opens*)

SPIKE   Yes, boss, what can I do?

TREET   Get my car out, Spike. Mr. Marlowe, here, is going to accompany us to the apartment of the late Wealthy Jacobus Pike. I think we have stumbled on a murder.

(*Music: Stab and out. Sound: Knocks on door*)

MARLOWE   I hope we are not too late, Mr. Treet.

(*Door opens*)

RUDY   Oh, it's you, Mr. Marlowe.

MARLOWE   Hello, Rudy, this is Mr. Treet, Chaser . . .

RUDY   Not the surly old investigator?

■ ■ ■

47

SPIKE   That's right, Bucko, and who might you be?

TREET   If I'm not mistaken, Spike, this is Rudy, Mr. Pike's valet.

MARLOWE   That's right, Mr. Treet.

RUDY   Oh, I've hoid a lot about you, Mr. Treet. Come in.

(*Door closes*)

MARLOWE   There he is, Mr. Chase. Over there on the floor where I found him.

TREET   The name is Treet, Marlowe.

SPIKE   He seems nervous, boss. Shall I frisk him?

TREET   No, that's not necessary, I have already seen to that. Oh, Rudy, will you ask Julia Pike, Wealthy's sister, to step in here, please?

SPIKE   Boss, Greg Marlowe, here, is a young playwright secretly in love with Julia, who dreams of a career on the stage.

TREET   Exactly, Spike. I want to question everybody.

MARLOWE   But, Mr. Treet, Julia doesn't have anything to do with . . .

(*Door opens*)

TREET   Ah, Miss Julia Pike?

JULIA   You sent for me, Mr. Chase?

TREET   Yes, come in, Julia. Sit down.

SPIKE   And the name is Lost, Miss Pike, not Chase.

(*Door closes*)

TREET   No, Spike, you're People, and I'm Treeter chasing lost vistas.

■ ■ ■

48

MARLOWE   Well, aren't you a little misted yourself, Trace?

RUDY   If you folks don't mind, I'll just step out to the kitchen.

SPIKE   Not so fast, Rudy. Mr. Trader here thinks you lose people.

TREET   Or at least we'll chase it that way for now.

JULIA   Mr. Loster, you have chosen a lot of treats in your career.

TREET   On the contrary, Julia, cheating is not tracing choosers.

SPIKE   And if anyone can lose my boss, Mr. Cheepful here can poop!

TREET   Thanks for the vote of treetle, Pete.

JULIA   I have a headache, Mr. Poet. May I chapel to the lost room and treat?

TREET   Not so fast, Julia. Spike, get my car.

SPIKE   Right, boss.

TREET   No one is to leave this room until I get back. In the meantime, you are all under suspicion. I think every one of you is lost.

   (*Music: Stab and out*)

SPIKE   But, boss, you left all the suspects back there at Wealthy Jacobus Pike's famous Broadway backer's apartment . . . What if they try to escape?

TREET   Exactly what I'm figuring, Spike. One of those persons—Julia Pike, sister of Wealthy Jacobus Pike, Rudy, his valet, or Greg Marlowe, handsome young playwright secretly in love with Julia (who dreams of a career on the stage)—is the guilty one.

■ ■ ■

49

SPIKE   Then it's some kind of a trap, boss?

TREET   Quiet, Spike!

SPIKE   What?

TREET   (*Whisper*) Act as if nothing has happened, Spike. I'm sure that someone is listening outside the door. I'll just walk over to the door quietly . . .

(*Door opens*)

SPIKE   Who is there, boss?

TREET   No one, Spike. I could have sworn— Spike, what are you doing with that gun?

SPIKE   Pointing it at you, boss.

TREET   But you can't mean that you, that you're . . .

SPIKE   That's right, boss. But just as soon as I rip off this mask (*effort*), you'll see that I'm not really your assistant, Spike, but I'm—

TREET   Julia Marlowe!

JULIA   Yes, Mr. Treet.

TREET   No one, Spike. I could have sworn— Spike, mask (*effort*), you'll see that I am really—

JULIA   Rudy! Mr. Pike's valet!

RUDY   At last we are together, in love as we are with each other!

JULIA   Rudy!

RUDY   Julia!

(*Fade in theme music under*)

BOB   And so another case from the files of Mr. Treet is marked solved. Listen next time when the surly old

■ ■ ■

investigator brings us "The Shanty With the Open Door on the Old Vacant Lot across the Railroad Tracks Murder Clue."

(*Music: Tag and out*)

■ ■ ■

lawrence fechtenberger, interstellar officer candidate

. . .

ANNOUNCER And now . . . the H. J. Flammish Company of Keswick, Ohio, makers of cotton-picking machines, presents . . . *Lawrence Fechtenberger, Interstellar Officer Candidate.*

(*Music: Space theme*)

BOSWORTH HARTLEY And here he is, the idol of millions of space-conscious American boys and girls . . . Lawrence Fechtenberger!

. . .

FECHTENBERGER   Lawrence Fechtenberger . . . reporting for duty!

(*Theme music up, then out*)

BOSWORTH HARTLEY   Before we join Lawrence and his serious, yet fun-loving, fellow officer candidates at the Interstellar Academy, a word from Messmore Tisdale . . .

TISDALE   Good day. This is Messmore Tisdale, speaking for the H. J. Flammish Company of Keswick, Ohio, makers of cotton-picking machines. The H. J. Flammish Company thinks more of its employees than it does of its business. It spends over $345,000 each year just to wrap the pickles separately in wax paper in the free hot lunches it serves every day. Here is Mr. Wilbur Trimble, an H. J. Flammish Company employee for forty-six years . . . Mr. Trimble.

TRIMBLE   I been working for the H. J. Flammish Company for forty-six years. They been good to me. Once, when I fell into a cotton-picking machine I was testing . . . when I got out of the hospital a year and a half later they had my suit all cleaned and pressed and mended, free of charge.

TISDALE   That's what I mean when I say that the H. J. Flammish Company thinks more of its employees than it does of its business. And now back to Bosworth Hartley.

HARTLEY   When we left Lawrence Fechtenberger, Interstellar Officer Candidate, he was talking to Officer Candidate Mug Mellish, who unbeknownst to the sterling lads of the Interstellar Academy, had been dishonorably discharged from the Mars Rocket School on the planet Mars for stealing plutonium. We hear them talking near the rocket landing platform . . .

■ ■ ■

FECHTENBERGER   Hello, Mug Mellish.

MELLISH   Hello, Fechtenberger.

FECHTENBERGER   A bit surly today, aren't you, Mellish?

MELLISH   If I want to be surly, that's my own affair.

FECHTENBERGER   Come, come, Officer Candidate Mellish. None of our other sterling lads are surly. Why be the exception that proves the rule?

MELLISH   You mind your own—

FECHTENBERGER   Tell you what. Let's try out this new rocket bomber with the atomic deicer on the prepodium.

MELLISH   All right, but I'll sneer about it all the way.

FECHTENBERGER   We'd better strap on our gas-ray guns just in case.

MELLISH   I got mine in my shoulder holster.

FECHTENBERGER   That's against regulations!

MELLISH   Who cares about regulations?

FECHTENBERGER   Well, let's go. Close the anti-electronic portholes.

   (*Sound: Electronic winch*)

FECHTENBERGER   Now desensitize the post-lateral starboard stabilizers.

   (*Sound: Mechanical*)

FECHTENBERGER   Now shut the door.

   (*Sound: Door shut*)

FECHTENBERGER   Ready, Officer Candidate Mellish?

MELLISH   Yeah.

■ ■ ■

FECHTENBERGER   Then we're off to the moon!

(Sound: Rocket takeoff, then settle down under. Music: Interstellar stuff)

FECHTENBERGER   Well, everything seems to be going jim dandy, O.C. Mellish.

MELLISH   That's what you think, Fechtenberger. Put your hands up.

FECHTENBERGER   What? What are you doing?

MELLISH   Never mind. Stick 'em up.

FECHTENBERGER   Okay, but this is a dastardly outrage.

MELLISH   And now . . . to change course.

(Sound: Change in rocket hum)

FECHTENBERGER   Mug! Mug, don't! Why, you are headed for . . . for . . .

BOSWORTH HARTLEY   Headed for what? Listen next time to *Lawrence Fechtenberger, Interstellar Officer Candidate* . . . and learn what happens when children fool around with machines.

(Music: Up, then under)

TISDALE   And this is Messmore Tisdale saying goodbye for the H. J. Flammish Company, cotton-picker manufacturers of Keswick, Ohio. If you need a cotton picker this year, won't you let us show you what we have? Thank you.

(Music: Up and out)

■ ■ ■

hard-luck
stories

. . .

Next week's Hard Luck Story is Bob's tailor.

RAY Once again, we've had our scouts searching the
railroad and bus stations around New York for
victims of misfortune who need a helping hand from
our generous Bob and Ray organization. And, Bob,
I see that you have one of those pathetic creatures
there at the microphone with you now.

BOB Yes, I have, Ray. This miserable specimen is Mrs.
Wanda Stapp of Collinsville, Illinois. And according
to the report from our Bob and Ray scout, you

were found loping along Park Avenue on all fours, Mrs. Stapp. Is that correct?

STAPP   (*Falsetto*) Well, I don't know that I'm too crazy about your choice of words there. I do have a back condition that causes me to walk in a bent-over position. But I wouldn't call that loping along on all fours.

BOB   Well, I'm sure that the young man who wrote up this report intended no offense. He was just using a descriptive phrase to indicate that you looked like something less than human.

STAPP   Well, I guess it does sound better when you put it that way. I don't know. I'm just so sensitive about it. It's been almost a month since my back locked on me. I was stooping to pick up a pari-mutuel ticket at the track in East St. Louis.

BOB   I see. You dropped a winning ticket—and when you bent over to get it, you couldn't straighten up again. Is that it?

STAPP   Well, that's not exactly it, no. It was somebody else who dropped the ticket I was trying to pick up.

BOB   Well, that part is not too important. It's your—

STAPP   Well, it *is* important because the person who dropped the ticket was the one who caught me across the back of the neck with a judo chop. I haven't been able to straighten up since. It's going to take a New York specialist to bring me out of this—once you fine people have lent a helping hand.

BOB   Well, a helping hand is indeed what we're offering to you, Mrs. Stapp. Thanks to the generous Bob and Ray organization, you're going to get a free trip to the top of the Statue of Liberty for a panoramic view of Manhattan.

■ ■ ■

STAPP   Well, that's ridiculous. All bent over this way, I'll just get a panoramic view of the bottom of the statue.

BOB   Please don't try to express your gratitude, ma'am. We're here to help . . . Now moving along to our next downtrodden guest with a hard-luck story to tell, here is Mr. Clifton Nefty of Bay City, Michigan. And, sir, I understand that our Bob and Ray scouts found you sitting on a curb down on Wall Street.

NEFTY   That's right. I was wearing this same frayed Argyle sweater and knickers that I have on now. And I was trying to sell my stock holdings to anyone there on the street who might be interested.

BOB   Well, that's what your card states. But wouldn't any of the brokerage houses let you come inside to sell your securities?

NEFTY   Not these particular securities, no. You see, I made a lot of money during World War II. And I plowed it all into sound investments right after V-J Day. I went into Packard Motors, Crosley Radio, and also several large interurban and streetcar lines in the Midwest.

BOB   Well, you didn't exactly pick the firms that were destined to prosper in the postwar era, did you?

NEFTY   No. My business stupidity has been quite a source of grief to me. Judging from the two sales I made on Wall Street this morning, I'd say I've run a ten-million-dollar fortune into about three dollars and seventy-five cents.

BOB   Well, your pathetic story of a fortune made and lost has touched us all deeply. And our generous Bob and Ray organization wants you to have this lovely set of new plastic seat covers for your Edsel.

■ ■ ■

NEFTY How did you know I drive an Edsel? I didn't tell anybody around here.

BOB You didn't have to, sir. It just seemed inevitable . . . And now here with today's final tear-jerker is Mrs. Nola Krowdish of Erie, Pennsylvania. Mrs. Krowdish, I understand that yours is a tragic story of coming to New York to seek psychiatric help.

KROWDISH No, not in the beginning. I really came to New York to get a lock of Walter Cronkite's mustache. But after I was caught coming at him with a scissors, the judge told me I'd have to seek psychiatric help within seventy-two hours or go to the pokey.

BOB Well, I know that's a terrible alternative for a person like yourself who's virtually penniless. And to help you in your moment of need, our generous Bob and Ray organization wants you to have this lovely set of genuine bone-handled carving knives.

KROWDISH Well, that's awful. If they catch me within ten miles of Walter Cronkite with these things, I'm a dead pigeon.

BOB You're entirely welcome. We knew you'd be pleased.

■ ■ ■

mary mcgoon's recipe for frozen ginger ale salad

■ ■ ■

MARY Hello, everyone. This is Mary McGoon. It's so good to talk to you all again. It's time that we all talk of food and so forth. I thought I should like to talk briefly about a favorite salad of mine. I know that salads are playing an ever-increasing role in the serving of foods in fine restaurants. That's why I have, today, a favorite recipe of mine that I'd like to give you all now. It's called frozen ginger ale salad, and this is how I make it.

■ ■ ■

First, you take a huge crock and fill it with the contents of a quart bottle of ginger ale. (Either pale or golden, it makes no difference.) You just pour it in. Then I take a head of lettuce, Boston or romaine or iceberg, and shred that and put that into the crock containing the ginger ale. Then I swish it all around until it's thoroughly swished. I get to giggling on that. It's so much fun. You can wear a rubber glove, if you choose.

After it's thoroughly swished, I take a marshmallow and cube it. And that will keep you busy. After that's been cubed, friends, you put that in, too. Then I take a chocolate bar with almonds, and I remove the almonds and break the chocolate into little bits and put that in, too. Then I swish it all together. When it's completely swished and settles down a little in the crock, I pour it off into a mold made in the likeness of a dear friend of mine. Then I take it up and put it into the freezing compartment of my refrigerator. After it's hard, and you can tell when it's hard because it will be hard when you touch it, you take it out and chip into individual servings. Serve it with Argyle sox sauce and garnish with pimento. Well, that's about it. You serve that to your family and I know they will really appreciate it. It's a dish fit for a king.

■ ■ ■

squad car 119

...

"You mean it's illegal?"

ANNOUNCER   And now the Monongahela Metal Foundry, maker of extra shiny steel ingots for home and office use, invites you to ride with the men of *Squad Car 119*.

(Dramatic theme music. Establish and under for)

FINCH   My name's Sam Finch. Me and my partner, Ralph R. Kruger, Jr., are the unsung heroes of the police force. We ride a prowl car at night—winter, summer, spring, Labor Day—always on the lookout

...

for trouble. The other evening, we'd just gone on duty when my partner, Ralph R. Kruger, Jr., turned to me and said—

(*Music out*)

KRUGER   Sure be glad when this night's over, Sam. I haven't had any sleep in two days. Just lie there trying to think of a town in Washington that begins with "W."

FINCH   What do you need to know that for?

KRUGER   Well, I don't need to know it, Sam. It's just a way to get to sleep. You know, think of a town in every state that begins with the same letter as the state.

FINCH   You mean like Philadelphia, Pennsylvania?

KRUGER   No, Sam—the *same* letter. Honolulu, Hawaii . . . Anchorage, Alaska . . . Milwaukee, Minnesota . . . like that.

FINCH   Milwaukee's not in Minnesota, Ralph R. Kruger, Jr.

KRUGER   Really? Well, there's some town up there next to St. Paul. I'll try to stay awake and think of it.

RADIO   Calling Car 119. Car 119. Go to the corner of Rossmore and LaBrea to meet the officers from Unit 71 and help apprehend a suspect.

KRUGER   Gee, they want us to meet the guys from Unit 71, Sam. Have we ever met them before?

FINCH   I don't think so. Sure would have worn my good suit if I'd known we were going to be meeting new people.

KRUGER   I hate meeting people for the first time. Makes my palms get sweaty.

■ ■ ■

63

FINCH   I know what you mean. I never know what to say to them. Wearing this rumpled suit just makes it worse.

KRUGER   With me, the bad part is having to shake hands when my palms are sweaty. New people always notice sweaty palms right off.

FINCH   Yeah. But you've got a knack with words, Ralph R. I never know what to say.

KRUGER   Suppose I talk to them while you shake hands. Then they won't know I've got sweaty palms.

FINCH   They'll still see my rumpled suit, though. Maybe if I just stayed in the car and reached out the window to shake hands.

KRUGER   That might work. Boy, I sure hate meeting new people for the first time.

RADIO   Car 119! Car 119! Disregard that call to meet Unit 71 and help apprehend a suspect. The situation is now under control. The suspect has been apprehended, booked and brought to trial. In one moment, the results of that trial . . .

ANNOUNCER   While we're waiting to hear the outcome of this week's exciting case, just a brief word from the Monongahela Metal Foundry. Ladies, you know how ashamed you feel to serve dinner guests when there are dull, corroded steel ingots piled up on the table. That's why the folks at Monongahela have introduced new, extra shiny ingots for home and office use. You'll be proud to display them along with your finest china and silverware. So ask about them at your local Monongahela Foundry salesroom today.

RADIO   . . . The suspect apprehended in that case at Rossmore and LaBrea was convicted on three

■ ■ ■

counts of being apprehended and one count of being a suspect. Apprehended suspects are punished under state law by a term of not less than five years in the correctional institution at Soledad.

(Theme music. Establish and under for)

ANNOUNCER And so another desperate criminal is brought to justice by the unsung heroes of the police force—the men who ride the squad cars at night.

(Theme up briefly and then out)

bulletin

...

Here is an additional supplementary bulletin from the Office of Fluctuation Control, Bureau of Edible Condiments; Soluble, Insoluble, and Indigestible Fats and Glutinous Derivatives, Washington, D.C. Correction to correction of Directive 943456201: In the aforementioned directive, the quotation on ground hogmeat, formerly groundhog meat, should read "chopped hogmeat."

lucky
phone call

...

BOB   Here we go to dial Oakland, California, selected scientifically for our Bob and Ray Lucky Phone Call. Let's hope our lucky recipient is home to receive our award.

(*Sound: Dialing phone, phone buzz, pickup of phone*)

VOICE   Hello?

BOB   Hello, is this Oakland 3-2135?

■ ■ ■

VOICE   Let me check . . . yeah, this is it.

BOB   Well, we have the right number, let's hope we have the right man. This is Bob and Ray calling from New York, sir. It's our lucky phone call if you are Mr. G. E. Porgy. Is that right, sir?

PORGY   That's right, I am.

BOB   Congratulations, you have received the Bob and Ray Lucky Phone Call. Tell us a little bit about yourself, Mr. Porgy. What's your first name?

PORGY   George. What I do, I'm working at the Top of the Roof restaurant in San Francisco.

BOB   I've been there many times. Are you a waiter?

PORGY   I'm a dessert man. I make mostly puddings and pies. Is this Ray?

BOB   No, this is Bob.

PORGY   I can never tell you fellows apart.

BOB   George E. Porgy, can you tell us how long you have been at the Top of the Roof, and how long you have been in the dessert business?

PORGY   I've been making pudding and pies ever since I got out of cooks and bakers school in the service in World War I.

BOB   Do you kiss the waitresses and make them cry?

PORGY   Ha-ha. They giggle, they giggle. When I come out of the kitchen to kiss one of the waitresses or the patrons, they all kind of giggle and laugh.

BOB   Well, it's the personal touch that has endeared you and the Top of the Roof restaurant . . .

PORGY   The whole gang here including the dishwasher and the salad man are wondering what I am going

■ ■ ■

to get because of the Lucky Phone Call. They are all pretty excited.

BOB   Right.

PORGY   What time is it back there?

BOB   Three hours' difference.

PORGY   Wow!

BOB   George, nice to talk to you and congratulations again on being our Lucky Phone Call recipient. The first one of this month, in fact.

PORGY   What will I get? They are all wondering.

BOB   You are going to get a season pass to the Bob and Ray Show. You can come to any one or to all, if you would rather, here at the studio.

PORGY   (*Pause*) If you ever come out here . . .

BOB   So long to Mr. George E. Porgy in Oakland, Calif—

PORGY   . . . I'll punch you right in your nose. I wish you would fly out at my expense.

BOB   That's about all the time we have for the phone call.

PORGY   (*To his co-workers*) I'm gonna get a season pass to those bums!

BOB   Now he is telling the good news to those folks out there. So long, sir, and so much for this Lucky Phone Call!

■ ■ ■

lumber dealers'
award

...

BOB We're mighty proud to have been named by the
North Dakota Lumber Dealers as the best radio
comedy team of 1974. And here to present us with
the award is the radio/television editor of the *North
Dakota Lumber Dealers' Review*, Mr. Ramses
Fletch . . . Sir, it's nice of you to come all the way
from Bismarck to make the presentation.

FLETCH Well, the lumber dealers back home felt that
they could afford to sponsor this trip for me. This

...

past year was a pretty good one for lumber in North Dakota.

BOB   I'm certainly glad to hear that, and I know Ray is too.

FLETCH   There's been a slight decline in the sale of ash and walnut, but the dealers in North Dakota are enjoying the greatest mahogany boom in their history.

BOB   That so?

FLETCH   Yes . . . I was hoping to have our 1973 fourth-quarter sales figures in time for this broadcast, but a few outlying reports haven't come in. I can say, however, that our dealers are running several million board feet ahead of the comparable period in 1972.

BOB   Now, you are the radio/television editor for the *Lumber Dealers' Review* up in North Dakota, is that right?

FLETCH   Yes, I write a monthly column for our publication, entitled "Radio and Television Highlights."

BOB   You review all of the new shows that go on the air, I suppose.

FLETCH   No, I review all of the new radio and television cabinets. After all, that's what the lumber dealers are most interested in—wooden cabinets.

BOB   I suppose they would be.

FLETCH   For instance, if a set manufacturer switches from walnut to blond mahogany in his cabinets . . . that causes quite a ripple in the lumber business.

BOB   Sort of indicates a trend, doesn't it?

FLETCH   Trend toward what?

■ ■ ■

BOB   A trend toward blond mahogany.

FLETCH   Well, I'd have to check our figures on that.

BOB   I see. Well now, would you tell us a little bit about this award that you've come to present today?

FLETCH   Well, once each year, in my column "Radio and Television Highlights," I select what I believe to be the best shows in each category, and the lumber dealers have a number of plaques made up out of heavy two-inch oak for presentation to the winners.

BOB   And I see you're holding up our plaque right there. I wonder if you'd read the inscription, would you?

FLETCH   I'd be happy to. The North Dakota Lumber Dealers' Association, composed of Morgan's Lumberyard in Bismarck; the Apex Lumber and Hardware Company in Grand Forks; Snyder, Your Lumberman, in Jamestown . . .

BOB   Just a minute, Mr. Fletch. You're not going to read off the name of every lumber dealer in North Dakota, are you?

FLETCH   Well, there's only about sixty of them . . .

BOB   We don't have time for all those names. Would you just move along to the citation, please?

FLETCH   Well, okay. The Lumber Dealers of North Dakota present this award for the best radio comedy of 1974 to you . . . Gene and Glenn.

BOB   Gene and Glenn? We're not Gene and Glenn . . . we're Bob and Ray, Mr. Fletch.

FLETCH   I'm terribly sorry.

BOB   I'm Bob, and that's Ray over there.

■ ■ ■

FLETCH   I must have walked into the wrong studio! Could you tell me where I could find Gene and Glenn?

BOB   I'm afraid not. I don't think they've been on the air for some time.

FLETCH   There's a station in Fargo that carries them every day, sponsored by Twenty Grand Cigarettes.

BOB   That couldn't be. They haven't made those since way back before World War II.

FLETCH   That's funny . . . We must get a delayed broadcast of some kind back home.

■ ■ ■

mr. science

∎ ∎ ∎

RAY Now, as a public service paid for by the Philanthropic Council to Make Things Nicer, we invite
you to spend another educational session with the
idol of the nation's youngsters—Mr. Science. As
we look in on the modern, well-equipped laboratory
today, we see that little Jimmy Schwab is just ar-
riving to watch Mr. Science perform his latest
fascinating experiment.

(Sound: Door slam)

∎ ∎ ∎

MR. SCIENCE   Oh, hello there, Jimmy. You're just in time to watch me perform my latest fascinating experiment.

JIMMY   Gee willikers, Mr. Science. I'm always fascinated by your fascinating experiments. Which one are you going to perform today?

MR. SCIENCE   Well, Jimmy, today we're going to observe what happens when we boil water right here in the laboratory.

JIMMY   Great day in the morning, Mr. Science! . . . I don't understand what you're talking about.

MR. SCIENCE   Well, it's really not as complicated as it sounds. You see, each chemical property has its own particular temperature point at which it changes from a liquid to a gas. And loosely defined, steam is the form of gaseous vapor that water is converted into when we heat it to 212 degrees.

JIMMY   Holy mackerel, Mr. Science. I don't understand that even worse than what you said the first time.

MR. SCIENCE   Well, don't worry about it, son. I'm sure it'll all become very clear to you after you've observed today's experiment. Now, in order to see what happens when we bring water to the boiling point, we must first prepare our laboratory equipment to heat it to 212 degrees.

JIMMY   Gosh-all hemlock, Mr. Science. What's that piece of laboratory equipment you're lighting with a match?

MR. SCIENCE   This device is called a candle, Jimmy.

JIMMY   A candle! Holy suffering catfish. Wait'll I tell all the kids at school I've seen one of those.

■ ■ ■

MR. SCIENCE   Now, just try to keep your enthusiasm under control, boy. We still haven't gotten to the most amazing part. Watch what happens when I hold this test tube filled with water over the lighted candle.

JIMMY   Golly Moses, Mr. Science! Nothing happened at all.

MR. SCIENCE   Well, that's only because the water hasn't been heated quite long enough yet. Remember, I told you that all chemical properties are converted from liquid to vapor once their temperature rises sufficiently.

JIMMY   Great Jumping Jehoshaphat! The water's starting to get all bubbling on top. I guess doing that instead of turning into a vapor offers conclusive proof that water's not a chemical property. Right, Mr. Science?

MR. SCIENCE   No. That's not quite correct, Jimmy. You see, those bubbles indicate that the water is starting to boil. And now, if you'll look closely, you can see steam beginning to rise from the test tube.

JIMMY   Oh, wowie-two-shoes! But that stuff sure looks an awful lot like the smoke that was rising from the candle. You wouldn't try to slip me the old rubber peach just because I'm a gullible child, would you, Mr. Science?

MR. SCIENCE   No. Of course not, Jimmy. Notice how my hand gets wet when I pass it through the cloud of steam like this. And that means the vapor has converted itself back into water again.

JIMMY   Boy oh boy, your hand's sure wet, all right, Mr. Science. I feel as though one of nature's eternal secrets has just been unlocked before my very eyes.

■ ■ ■

MR. SCIENCE   That's very cleverly phrased, Jimmy. And—

JIMMY   I'll bet this little bottle would get equally wet if I passed it through the cloud of steam.

MR. SCIENCE   No. Don't do that, Jimmy. The contents of that bottle must never be exposed to heat! Keep it away from here, boy!

JIMMY   But I only want to see if the outside of the bottle will—

(*Sound: Explosion*)

ANNOUNCER   Mr. Science has been brought to you as a public service paid for by the Philanthropic Council to Make Things Nicer. Today's broadcast was the last in our current series.

■ ■ ■

the
piel brothers:
bert's
offenses

•••

BERT   This is Bert Piel . . .

HARRY   And this is Harry Piel.

BERT   Piels tastes best of all, because it's the driest of
all. Remember that, viewers.

HARRY   Excuse me, Bert. Friends, my brother is so enthusiastic over our wonderful beer that . . . he sometimes—without meaning to—offends an occasional
viewer.

•••

BERT   Offends?

HARRY   I'm sorry, Bert. But we've had some letters . . .
and a lady in New Jersey says you . . .

BERT   (*Hurt*) Wha–what?

HARRY   I'm sorry. You go ahead.

BERT   No, no. I've tried to tell people how delicious our
beer is . . . How it'll bring happiness into their nice
homes. Somehow I've offended. You tell them,
Harry. They like you. You're personable. I'm offen-
sive . . . Goodbye, consumers.

(*Sound: Footsteps out, door slams*)

HARRY   I'm sorry he's so sensitive. I never should have—

(*Sound: Gunshot outside*)

HARRY   Bert!!

(*Sound: Door opens and footsteps in*)

BERT   Bull's-eye! Proof Piels aims for dryness . . . and
we don't miss!

HARRY   Well, as Bert, thank goodness, says . . . if you
taste it and smack your lips, it's a product of Piel
Brothers, most likely.

BERT   Unquestionably, Harry!

■ ■ ■

anxiety

...

ANNOUNCER And now it's time for another story of
drama and human emotion—a tale well designed
to keep you in . . . *Anxiety!*

(Sound: Stinger)

ANNOUNCER Here to set the stage for this week's yarn
is the famous lecturer and world traveler, Commander Neville Putney. Commander, I presume
that you've reached into your amazing file and

■ ■ ■

brought forth another tale well designed to keep our listeners in . . . Anxiety!

(*Sound: Stinger*)

PUTNEY (*British accent*) Indeed I have, young man. Like all my stories, this one is a true account of ordinary men and women leading ordinary lives, never dreaming that they are about to become enmeshed in a web of . . . Anxiety!

(*Sound: Stinger*)

PUTNEY One of the central figures in this week's tale was a young reservations clerk at the Greyhound bus station in Honolulu. Her name was Lorelei Leilanie. And as our story begins, Miss Leilanie is just putting down the phone on her desk. Terror is written all over her face as she turns to her immediate superior, Mr. Dockweiler, and says—

(*Sound: Background crowd noise*)

LEILANIE (*Falsetto*) Good grief, Mr. Dockweiler. I feel as if there's terror written all over my face. An anonymous caller just phoned from New York to say there's a bomb in the bus station timed to go off at nine o'clock.

DOCKWEILER Good grief, Miss Leilanie. We must get the Honolulu police bomb squad in on this matter at once.

LEILANIE There's no time for that now. Look at the giant clock on the bus station wall. It's barely four minutes to nine.

DOCKWEILER Good grief, you're right. Then our only hope is to herd these thousands of milling passengers outside to safety before the explosion.

LEILAINE But can't you understand—there's no time

■ ■ ■

83

for that. We have only three minutes left. And that bomb must be hidden in one of those five hundred and eighty-five lockers that run the full length of the wall over there.

DOCKWEILER Good grief, Miss Leilanie. Surely you can't be suggesting that the two of us search five hundred and eighty-five lockers in less than three minutes. Why, that figures out to—Let's see. Three goes into five once with two to carry—

LEILANIE There's no time for that sort of precise calculation now. All we can do is search as many lockers as we have time for, and hope that Lady Luck is on our side.

DOCKWEILER You're right, Miss Leilanie. The odds are at least a hundred to one against our opening the right locker in time. But if we're destined to be blown to smithereens, then let it be fate that decides this game of chance for us.

(*Sound: Stinger*)

ANNOUNCER Boy, that was one of your most spine-tingling stories yet, Commander. But you can't just leave us all in anxiety this way. Did Miss Leilanie and Mr. Dockweiler pick the right locker in the few fleeting seconds they had left to hunt for the bomb?

PUTNEY Well, as it developed, they had a good deal more time than they thought. If you'll recall, Miss Leilanie mentioned that the anonymous phone call came from New York. And of course when it's nine on the East Coast, it's only four in Honolulu. So they actually had five hours to find the bomb, which was ample time.

ANNOUNCER Well, that's ridiculous. They were going

■ ■ ■

by the clock on the Honolulu bus station wall. And it wouldn't have been set on New York time.

PUTNEY Well, perhaps the clock had stopped the night before and nobody noticed it. I do wish you wouldn't nit-pick this way at all the stories I draw forth from my amazing file. It might cause people to think that some of them aren't entirely factual.

ANNOUNCER Well, nobody in his right mind could believe that one. The whole idea of having it take place in the Greyhound bus station at Honolulu is absurd. Where could a person go on a Greyhound bus from there?

PUTNEY I didn't say anybody was taking a bus. I merely said that people were milling about the station. Now read your closing announcement, you cheeky young blighter.

ANNOUNCER Well, after that story I sure feel like a fool reading what's written down here.

PUTNEY Never mind your emotional problems. Just read it.

ANNOUNCER Well, okay . . . Friends, be sure to join us again next time when Commander Putney once more reaches into his incredible file of amazing true stories, and brings forth a tale well designed to keep you in . . . *Anxiety!*

(*Sound: Stinger*)

■ ■ ■

sun-drenched
acres

■ ■ ■

BOB I hope you younger listeners will bear with us for just a moment here while we take advantage of this opportunity to bring news of glorious hope to all of the senior citizens in our audience. Old-timers, that long-cherished dream of spending your golden years in balmy Florida can now come true at a cost that defies description.

RAY He speaks right, friends. After months of planning, choice lots in Bob and Ray's Sun-Drenched Acres

■ ■ ■

are off the drawing boards and on the open market, just waiting to be taken advantage of.

BOB Best of all, a far greater selection of building sites is still available than we had hoped. And as a result, you can now retire in comfort and stop being a drag on your relatives even if you are a nonveteran.

RAY Assuming you have approved credit.

BOB Exactly. But, neighbors, please don't let the incredible down payment lead you to believe that Bob and Ray's Sun-Drenched Acres is nothing more than undeveloped, raw land. Far from it. The attractive street signs are already in. And lovely, handcarved surveyors' stakes mark off each and every lot. Only running water, electricity, telephone lines and a means of access from the main highway have yet to be added.

RAY Now, if you are among the disappointed thousands who already have priced real estate in Florida and found it far beyond your means, you may be wondering how we can make it possible for you to buy land in Bob and Ray's Sun-Drenched Acres even if you are a nonveteran.

BOB Assuming you have approved credit.

RAY Right. Well, the answer is simple, friends. Most retirement communities are located along the coastline of Florida, where unscrupulous promoters have pushed real estate prices sky high. But our rough plans call for Bob and Ray's Sun-Drenched Acres to be constructed in the center of the state, where the fly-by-night operators have not yet taken over.

BOB In fact, where we've laid out this lovely proposed community, no one at all has yet taken over. You'll find the property in the same untouched, natural state it was in almost a century ago when the

■ ■ ■

Seminole Indians gave it back to the federal government.

RAY   Now, we certainly don't need to tell you how much more healthful it is to live in central Florida than along the drafty, windswept seacoast. But perhaps you aren't aware of all the added convenience of the location. Bob and Ray's Sun-Drenched Acres will be only a short twenty-minute drive from the Everglades National Park if a road is ever constructed to make the drive possible.

BOB   But even while you're waiting for the road to be put through, you'll find the community a virtual sportsman's paradise. Many enthusiastic residents of the area tell us that they while away carefree hours shooting alligators right from their own front porch. And where else but in low-lying bottom land such as this would it be possible, after a heavy rain, to go fishing in your attic?

RAY   Best of all, such torrential rains are not mere freaks of nature that leave you with many dry, arid days when your fishing equipment must remain in the closet. No, indeed. Authentic Weather Bureau records show that you can expect up to three hundred inches of rainfall a year at Bob and Ray's Sun-Drenched Acres.

BOB   Right. Fears of a water shortage can be banished forever once you move into this lovely planned community. And if by chance one of the area's frequent torrential cloudbursts should wash your dream home onto a neighboring lot, arrangements have been made to tow it back again at minimal cost.

RAY   Now, certainly, you'll want to reserve a building site in Bob and Ray's Sun-Drenched Acres while a good selection remains. We believe that some corner

■ ■ ■

lots may even still be available, although we can't be sure, of course, until we know where the streets are located. But in any event there isn't a moment to lose.

BOB   Avoid disappointment by getting your request for information in the mail today. Just send it to Bob and Ray, Drenched, New York.

RAY   That address again: Bob and Ray, Drenched, New York.

■ ■ ■

blimmix

■ ■ ■

(Blimmix *theme music. Establish and under for*)

ANNOUNCER   And now Jungle Haven, the last roadside
zoo still operating on Interstate Five with real rac-
coons, invites you to join us for more thrilling action
in the life of . . . *Blimmix.*

(*Theme music up briefly and then fade for*)

BLIMMIX   My name's Joe Blimmix. I'm a private investigator. One evening last week, I was working
late at the office trying to decide which top to put

■ ■ ■

on my convertible. Suddenly, a knock on the door made me suspect that somebody might be outside. So I did the only thing I could. I said, "Come in!"

(*Sound: Door opens and closes*)

THUG   Good evening. I'm sorry to disturb you at this hour, sir, but I have a work order here to beat the stuffings out of a Joe Blimmix at this address. I wonder if you could tell me where to find him.

BLIMMIX   I'm Joe Blimmix. Who sent you here?

THUG   Gee, I'm not really sure. Maybe I've got the client's name on the bill of lading here. Let me check. (*Pause*) Yeah. Here it is. One fifty-dollar clobbering ordered by Big Dominick Lufsko.

BLIMMIX   Big Dom, huh? That figures. But I thought I knew all of his boys, and I don't remember seeing you around before.

THUG   Oh, I'm not one of his boys. I'm with Rent-a-Thug, Incorporated. A lot of the syndicate people are letting their regular hoodlums go and utilizing our service for machine-gunnings and roughing up and things like that. It saves all the bookwork that goes with having full-time employees.

BLIMMIX   Yeah. I can see how it would. No withholding tax or Social Security contributions or any of that sort of thing.

THUG   That's right. And then, too, your full-time mobsters all want pension plans and health insurance now. So it's really more economical in the long run just to call us over at Rent-a-Thug when you want a job done.

BLIMMIX   I'll remember that.

THUG   I hope you'll be able to after I finish with you.

■ ■ ■

A fifty-dollar clobbering really shakes up a person's brains. Now, if you'll just sign here to acknowledge receipt of what you've got coming to you.

BLIMMIX   But you haven't done anything to me yet.

THUG   I know. But you won't be able to sign after I'm finished with you. So just do it now on Line 31 there, please.

BLIMMIX   Okay. But I hope this isn't going to take long. I haven't even had dinner yet.

THUG   Oh, it'll only take a jiffy. I've got my brass knuckles and other equipment right here in the toolbox. That's one thing you've got to say for Rent-a-Thug. They never dispatch a man without the tools he needs to do a topnotch pummeling.

BLIMMIX   Well, suppose I decide I didn't especially want a pummeling.

THUG   I'm afraid you can't do that now, sir. You've already signed the receipt saying you got one. And we're certainly not the type of firm that takes a client's money and then fails to deliver. So just try to brace yourself and let me do what I got paid for.

BLIMMIX   Well, okay—since I've made the commitment. Is there anyplace special you want me to stand?

THUG   Just move a little to your right, please. No need to risk splitting your skull on the corner of the desk when you go down. That's not even included in a fifty-dollar clobbering. There. That's good. Now just relax to cut down on the broken bones. That's my boy. Perfect. Here we go.

(*Sound: Prolonged scuffling, furniture breaking*)

THUG   There. That should do it. Thank you very much, sir, and a pleasant evening to you.

■ ■ ■

(Sound: Footsteps and door closing)

BLIMMIX   After he left, I wasn't sure what to do. Normally, I would have called my client, but I didn't have any at the time. So I just marked the case "Unsolved" and stuck it away in the files—the files of Joe Blimmix, private investigator.

(Theme music. Establish and fade out)

■ ■ ■

wally ballou
at the
sewing contest

...

RAY   Now over to remote broadcaster Wally Ballou, who is standing by to bring you the finals of the world-famous Bob and Ray Sew-Off. Come in, please, Wally Ballou.

(*Sound of working sewing machines in background throughout*)

BALLOU   (*Off mike*) In your hat, lady, a beautiful picture . . .

VOICE   You're on now.

■ ■ ■

BALLOU   This is radio's highly regarded Wally Ballou speaking to you from the Annual Bob and Ray Sewing Contest. The ladies are using the Bob and Ray sewing machines. There are some fifty or sixty ladies here sewing away, busily putting the finishing touches on the items they have chosen to sew and enter in the competition for the big prize money. Here's a lady with a . . . what is that?

MISS FANG   Just a plain housedress I'm making.

BALLOU   Let's see, you are Miss Emma Fang. Where are you from, Miss Fang?

MISS FANG   I'm from Topeka, Kansas.

BALLOU   And you were flown here?

MISS FANG   I was flown here on the Bob and Ray Airline, the Route of the Open Cockpit.

BALLOU   Do you sew for your whole family?

MISS FANG   Yes, I make everyone's clothing except the old man's. He has to go to the fat man's shop.

BALLOU   He has a problem figure, kind of? Lots of luck with your housedress you're making. Now, here, a little further along the line, you are Mrs. Iris Bumgart?

BUMGART   That's right.

BALLOU   Could you tell us what your entry in the contest will be?

BUMGART   This is a slipcover.

BALLOU   For a sofa?

BUMGART   Yes.

BALLOU   Very nice. What is that—chintz?—you are making it out of? Is that the name of the material?

■ ■ ■

95

BUMGART   Yes, it is . . . Oww . . . I caught my finger there.

BALLOU   You have to be careful. Down here at the far end is an interesting sight. Here, amidst all these lady contestants, is a gentleman sitting at the sewing machine. I can't believe that he is an entrant in the Bob and Ray Sew-Off, but the card here says that he is. Sir, are you a contestant? (*Giggle*)

DRAPER   What are you laughing at? Yes, I am. My name is Wally Draper.

BALLOU   What do you do for a living, Mr. Draper?

DRAPER   I'm a mechanic. I like to sew; do you want to make something out of it?

BALLOU   No, no . . .

DRAPER   What are you winking at the engineer for?

BALLOU   I wasn't winking at the engineer. I was only getting a time signal from him. Can you tell us what you are making here?

DRAPER   An apron.

BALLOU   Something for your wife?

DRAPER   No, it's something for me. A special kind of apron—I can keep my tools here in the front.

BALLOU   I see . . . very handy to have around the machine shop.

DRAPER   Right, it is.

BALLOU   Have any of the ladies shown any antagonism toward you about being the only man in the contest?

DRAPER   They more or less ignored me, and that's the way I'd just as soon have it. Every time they go

■ ■ ■

96

by me, they go tsk, tsk, tsk—like that. I don't care, I just want to win the first prize . . . Are you winking at your engineer?

BALLOU   No, my engineer has just told me that our time is almost up. So again, good luck . . . Wait just a minute, they are going to make an address on the public address system. Let's see if we can pick it up . . .

PUBLIC ADDRESS   Attention, please stop the sewing! The board of directors has decided on the winner. It is Wally Draper of Gary, Indiana. Congratulations.

BALLOU   You heard it, ladies and gentlemen, the sissy won! the sissy won.

DRAPER   (*Mad*) What did you say? Wait a minute . . .

(*Pandemonium, smashing of furniture and mikes*)

RAY   (*Back at the studio*) That's unusual . . .

BOB   Wally walked right into that one!

■ ■ ■

mary
backstayge,
noble wife #1

■ ■ ■

From the Bob and Ray Show, *1952. The game of "Duplication" required peppermint patties, cards, checker and cribbage boards, and Audrey Meadows, who played Linda Lovely, the television equivalent of Mary Backstayge. She looks a little chilly.*

(*Theme music, in and under*)

WORD CARR   Mary Backstayge, Noble Wife! The story of America's Favorite Family of the Footlights and of their fight for security and happiness against the concrete heart of Broadway.

The story thus far . . .

Mary and Harry Backstayge, America's first family of the footlights, had just returned to their Skunk

■ ■ ■

Haven, Long Island, summer home from a mid-winter ski vacation at Foggy Bend, Vermont, with their next-door neighbor Calvin L. Hoogevin and their close friend Pop Beloved, stage doorman, when Greg Marlowe, young playwright (secretly in love with Mary) informed them of his plans to produce an early-morning television variety show calling for their "live" appearance as host and hostess of the network feature from 5:30 to 9:00 A.M. five days each week, in addition to continuing their eight performances each week in Greg's hit Broadway production, *Westchester Furioso,* a schedule to which they agreed before fully realizing the intense physical demands such a program would impose; eventually, the "Mr. and Mrs. Broadway" series was canceled by a network biggie, and Mary, Harry, Pop and Calvin accepted the invitation of their old friend, Lord Brandyshire, to spend a few weeks of relaxation at his palatial English country estate, Moorswind, during which visit they were entrusted with a brown paper bag containing something they were to guard with their very lives and take to Pepe Le Coco, a resident of the Casbah in Casablanca, whom they finally contacted following a series of adventures culminating in an uneventful return to the United States, only to find that Greg had sold the TV network on the idea of an African safari special.

The Backstayges did indeed go to Africa, and with Greg doing the camera work, returned with the TV special which the network scheduled for airing at seven A.M. on the Saturday following Thanksgiving. Now it's the following Monday, and Greg is calling the network V.P. to find out how the show did, rating-wise.

GREG   (*Quite somber*) Yes . . . well, I'll be in there

■ ■ ■

tomorrow . . . thank you, Duane, for the information. Goodbye.

HARRY You certainly wrote down a lot of numbers there, Greg.

GREG We didn't register very high in the ratings for that Saturday morning after Thanksgiving.

HARRY By that you mean we weren't equal to what the other networks were carrying?

MARY You mean those little cartoon things had a larger share of the audience?

POP I can't imagine a big television special like the Backstayges' safari show being beaten by animated cartoons.

CALVIN I know I forgot to tune in my TV set, so that was one viewer you didn't get.

POP Of course, there was one section of the show where I tap-danced for twenty minutes and Mary and Harry did Shakespeare. That might not compete with animation too well.

GREG I . . . errr . . .

HARRY Get on with it, Greg. You sound like you're holding something back. Give us the bad news.

GREG According to Duane, this is the first time in TV history a sampling showed no one was watching a special.

HARRY Ahuh, ahuh . . . By that you mean no one was watching the network we were on.

MARY You mean *no one* was watching our program?

GREG Precisely.

■ ■ ■

POP   Well, the engineers in the control room were watching, but I suppose they don't count in the rating.

GREG   (*Very slowly*) Here in New York, you had zero women between the ages of eighteen and twenty-five . . .

HARRY   Ahuh, ahuh . . .

GREG   . . . zero men between eighteen and twenty-five . . .

POP   How about the twenty-five to forty-nine group?

GREG   But in the twenty-five to forty-nine group, you had zero women . . .

HARRY   Ahuh, ahuh . . .

GREG   . . . and in the men . . .

MARY   I know, zero.

GREG   That's right, Mary.

HARRY   I saw you writing down all those zeroes, and I began to think you were just making a design, kinda doodling while he was telling you about the show.

GREG   Duane said he himself didn't watch the show. So (*Heaves a deep sigh*), I don't think TV is the answer for us.

HARRY   You mean they won't be asking us to produce another TV special?

CALVIN   I don't think that TV is the end-all. I mean, we can do lots of other things.

POP   True, there are other fields to conquer.

GREG   Like what?

HARRY   Yes, like what, Calvin?

■ ■ ■

POP   Yeah, like what?

CALVIN   Well, let's go into the restaurant business!

WORD CARR   And so, on hearing the bad news about their TV special, the Backstayges begin to think what to do next in the immediate future. Calvin suggested the restaurant business. You'll want to be here tomorrow when we'll hear Mary react and say . . .

MARY   Well, how do you cook scungilli?

WORD CARR   That's in the next exciting episode of *Mary Backstayge, Noble Wife*. Word Carr speaking.

■ ■ ■

impress-the-boss
kit

...

BOB Friends, does it seem like you're always being passed over at the office when the time comes for a promotion?

RAY Do you just go on doing the same job year after year, always efficient, but never conspicuous?

BOB Well, neighbors, it doesn't have to be that way. Quick success can be yours now, with the wonderful new Bob and Ray Impress-the-Boss Kit.

■ ■ ■

RAY   Here in one neat package is everything you need to convince your employer that you are the most diligent and valuable worker in the organization.

BOB   For example, the kit contains a generous three-ounce bottle of Bob and Ray eyedrops. These drops are guaranteed to make your eyes bloodshot, and lend credence to the story that you've been taking work home from the office and doing without sleep.

RAY   There's also a handy length of rubber tubing which can be run from your desk to the water cooler. Naturally, the boss will inquire about this . . . and a promotion is virtually insured when you inform him that you don't have time to leave your desk to get a drink of water!

BOB   Here, too, in this Impress-the-Boss Kit, is an ample jar of white make-up, guaranteed to give you a beautiful office pallor. After all, nobody's going to promote a healthy-looking specimen who appears to spend half his waking hours on the golf course.

RAY   And looking through the lower shelf of the kit, here I see that we have an atomizer filled with glycerine, which can be used to spray beads of sweat on your forehead. Every boss likes to see his employees sweating on the job.

BOB   A worried expression of concern can also go a long way toward winning you that much-wanted promotion—and the indelible make-up pencil included with each kit will enable you to have deeply etched furrows in your brow at all times.

RAY   Naturally, you'll want your employer to think that you don't have time to go out for lunch, and so each Bob and Ray Impress-the-Boss Kit contains an artificial plastic sandwich in your choice of either ham or cheese. You'll be proud to display

■ ■ ■

this handsome lifelike sandwich on your desk at all times.

BOB Yes, friends, there's just about everything in this kit to convince the boss that you are the eager beaver of the office staff.

RAY We could read endless letters here from our files telling how our kit enabled shipping clerks to become steel company presidents, and garbage men to become sanitation officials. But I'm sure the value of the kit is obvious to you without these testimonials.

BOB Certainly you'll want an Impress-the-Boss Kit for your very own, so why not act quickly and take advantage of our special bonus offer?

RAY If your order is postmarked before midnight tonight, you'll receive, at no additional charge, three simulated job-offer letters.

BOB These letters, which can be left around where the boss will see them, supposedly offer you jobs from other companies for much more money than you are now making.

RAY When the boss sees these letters, he'll realize that he must promote you quickly, in order to keep a valuable worker.

BOB Or he may fire you for disloyalty to his firm, but in any event you'll want to get more information about this offer before midnight tonight.

RAY Just address your inquiry to: "Gold Brick," in care of Bob and Ray, New York.

■ ■ ■

the
orderlies

■ ■ ■

(Dramatic-type theme music. Establish and under for)

ANNOUNCER   And now the Rotman Corporation, maker of fine buggy whips for more than nine centuries, presents *The Orderlies*—a dramatic behind-the-scenes glimpse of life in a big city hospital.

(Theme music up briefly and then out)

P.A.   Orderly Winecoop! Orderly Winecoop! Report at

■ ■ ■

once to Chief Orderly Schnellwell. Report to Chief Orderly Schnellwell.

(*Sound: Running footsteps*)

WINECOOP   You were anxious to see me, Chief Orderly Schnellwell?

SCHNELLWELL   I never get anxious about anything, Winecoop. Such emotions simply aren't tolerated among senior staff members of a big city hospital.

WINECOOP   Oh, I never meant to imply that you aren't hard as nails, Chief Orderly Schnellwell. And I apologize to the point of mortification for my poor choice of words.

SCHNELLWELL   What you should be apologizing for is your slowness in getting here. When I have you paged, that means I want to see you now, Orderly Winecoop—not seven or eight seconds from now.

WINECOOP   Well, I tried like crazy not to dawdle while I was climbing those twelve flights of stairs, Chief Orderly Schnellwell. But I guess that attack of nausea I had along the way slowed me down a little.

SCHNELLWELL   Winecoop, there's no room in the corps of orderlies for a man who gets nauseous simply because he's surrounded by the sight of blood and the sound of screaming patients.

WINECOOP   Oh, it wasn't the blood or screaming that got to me, your eminence. I had to run past the hospital kitchen to get here, and the smell of that awful food we serve would choke a horse.

SCHNELLWELL   It's a pity you feel that way, Winecoop —especially when you're talking about dietetic food that's been prescribed by doctors who have the power to assign you some very unpleasant duties. (*Chuckles*)

■ ■ ■

WINECOOP   Oh, no! Not the kitchen detail! Please don't let them do that to me, Chief Orderly Schnellwell. I'd crack up. I just know I would.

SCHNELLWELL   I don't know what makes you think I'd use my influence to save you from a lifetime of smelling mashed turnips, Winecoop. I already have a misconduct report here on my desk that makes some very serious allegations about you.

WINECOOP   Gee, I can't imagine what would prompt anybody to fink on me. I never commit any transgressions as I go about my menial chores here at a big city hospital.

SCHNELLWELL   No transgressions, eh? And what about the fact that you brazenly failed to page doctors over the public address system between two and four this morning as you were supposed to?

WINECOOP   Well, that wasn't real paging for real doctors that I was assigned to do. You told me yourself that you just made up some names for me to blab over the P.A. system in the middle of the night.

SCHNELLWELL   And so you just took it upon yourself not to carry out the mission because the doctors you were supposed to page are fictitious. Is that it?

WINECOOP   Well, it did seem kind of silly to page doctors who don't exist. Besides, having that raucous P.A. system going all night keeps the patients awake.

SCHNELLWELL   And of course it never occurred to you that when sick people don't get their proper rest, they have to recuperate here longer at ninety-three dollars a day.

WINECOOP   Oh, gosh no. That never occurred to me (*Starting to cry*) How could I have ever thought of

■ ■ ■

myself as a dedicated orderly? Even a green rookie knows better than to put the welfare of the patients ahead of the hospital's financial success. I'm a disgrace to the uniform I wear.

SCHNELLWELL   Now, don't be too hard on yourself, Winecoop. You were only acting out of ignorance and stupidity—not malice. And there's still time to rectify your mistake.

WINECOOP   You mean you're going to give me a second chance? Gee, you're a peach. And I promise I'll scream my lungs out over that P.A. system all night tonight. Nobody will get a wink of sleep.

SCHNELLWELL   Now you're speaking with the cruel inhumanity that can make you a credit to your profession, Winecoop. And I have a hunch that the day may soon be coming when I'll be proud to call you a colleague.

(*Theme music. Establish and under for*)

ANNOUNCER   And so, armed only with courage, perseverance and the will to commit atrocities against his fellow-man, the hospital orderly goes forth to do battle against medical progress. Be sure to join us next time when the Rotman Corporation, maker of fine buggy whips for more than nine centuries, will present another thrilling story of . . . *The Orderlies*.

(*Theme music up briefly and then out*)

■ ■ ■

tippy
the
wonder dog

. . .

(*Theme music. Establish and fade for*)

ANNOUNCER   And now Mushies—the great new cereal
that gets soggy even without milk or cream—brings
you another exciting story of adventure starring
Tippy the Wonder Dog.

(*Sound: Dog bark*)

ANNOUNCER   As we look in on the isolated cabin of
Grandpa Witherspoon today, we find that a hurri-

. . .

cane warning has been posted throughout the valley. Gramps is lying on his cot with the blanket pulled up—to shield himself from the approaching storm. Meanwhile, little Jasper stands in the front window —watching the rain and wind mount to a furious intensity. Suddenly, the boy turns and speaks . . .

BOY   It sure is blowing hard out there, Gramps.

GRAMPS   Consarn it all! I know it's blowing hard out there. And the storm is going to smash all the windows in this house before that fool dog of yours gets back with the lumber I need to board them up.

BOY   Oh, you don't need to have a moment's concern about that, Gramps. Tipp's always at his best in time of disaster. He'll be here with the lumber any minute now. He's the finest, smartest dog in the whole wide world.

GRAMPS   Well, consarn it all! What's keeping him? I already did the hard part—measuring the windows and tying a note around the fool dog's neck saying how many board feet of timber I needed.

BOY   Well, I guess Tippy might have stopped just long enough to double-check your figures. But I know he'll be here soon. He's the greatest, smartest dog in the whole wide world.

GRAMPS   Well, consarn it all! There was nothing to double-check but a simple column of figures. And I sent that fool dog to the lumberyard three days ago.

BOY   Ahoy! I think I see him coming up the road now, Gramps. (*Door opens and wind blowing*) Here, Tippy, Tippy, Tippy.

(*Door shuts and wind out*)

■ ■ ■

GRAMPS   Consarn it all! Where'd he put the lumber? I've got to get to work.

BOY   Sorry, Gramps, but that wasn't Tippy I saw. It was just the Shawmuts' beagle headed home with a can of kerosene—in case the electric lights go out.

GRAMPS   Consarn it all! Every other dog around here can make it through an eighty-mile-an-hour wind to do a simple errand. But that fool Tippy's probably taken cover in a hollow tree someplace.

BOY   For shame, Gramps. You know Tippy would never put his personal safety ahead of ours. He's the grandest, smartest—Wait! I see him coming now. (*Door opens and wind blowing*) Here, Tippy, Tippy, Tippy.

(*Door shuts and wind out*)

GRAMPS   Well, consarn it all! Hand me my rain slicker and I'll start boarding up the windows.

BOY   Not yet, Gramps. That wasn't Tippy after all. It was only that little mixed breed of the Kippermans. He was headed up that way with a coil of rope to lash down their farm implements.

GRAMPS   Consarn it all! That mutt's not worth what it costs to feed him. But he's still a darn sight smarter than that fool Tippy.

BOY   Gee whiz, Gramps. You shouldn't let your mounting fear cause you to say terrible things like that. Tippy's the swellest, smartest— Wait! I see him for sure now—staggering up the path through the howling gale to save us in the nick of time. (*Door opens and wind blowing*) Come on in, Tippy. That's a fine dog.

(*Door shuts and wind out*)

■ ■ ■

GRAMPS   Well, consarn it all! Where'd he put the lumber? On the porch?

BOY   He didn't bring any lumber, Gramps. I guess he had all he could handle carrying this old pie pan I used to throw for him to fetch.

GRAMPS   Consarn it all! I'm going to whirl that fool dog around by his tail and then send him flying into the next county.

BOY   No! Wait, Gramps! Don't you understand? Tippy's trying to show us that we can use this old pie pan for a rain gauge. And then when our readings show that the rain has stopped, we'll know that the hurricane is over. Boy! It really took some clever thinking for Tippy to solve our problem that way. But it's just like I told you. He's the brightest, smartest dog in the whole wide world.

(Theme music. Establish and under for)

ANNOUNCER   Today's fantastic story of adventure has been brought to you by Mushies—the great new cereal that gets soggy even without milk or cream. Join us again soon for more incredible action starring . . . Tippy the Wonder Dog.

(Theme music up briefly and then out)

■ ■ ■

mary backstayge, noble wife #2

■ ■ ■

Cloris Leachman, here helping us give a weather report, later replaced Audrey Meadows as Linda Lovely.

(*Music: Up and under*)

WORD CARR   Mary Backstayge, Noble Wife! The story of America's Favorite Family of the Footlights and of their fight for security and happiness against the concrete heart of Broadway. Yesterday, Mary, Harry, Pop and Calvin were contemplating opening a fast-food restaurant when they were unexpectedly visited by a Mr. Micklebar Nelson, who offered them a fast-food franchise business specializing in different kinds of toast. Now, sometime later, our

■ ■ ■

friends discuss the steps to be taken before opening Skunk Haven's first House of Toast.

(*Music: Out*)

CALVIN   There's one thing about toast . . .

HARRY   What's that, Calvin?

CALVIN   You can serve a thick shake with it. That's the secret.

HARRY   Or you can serve almost anything with it. The beauty of this idea is that we don't have to keep a lot of kinds of food on hand. Bread is the principal ingredient.

CALVIN   It's the staff of life, the Mother-of-Me always says.

POP   And it will make things easier in the kitchen, 'cause almost anybody can make toast.

MARY   I'm sure that Nelson has the machinery so that the toast will have a uniform brownness. You don't want to serve a black or burnt-edge toast.

HARRY   There will be all kinds too. Mr. Nelson said he would show us how to go about this. He claims to have had considerable success with this franchise on the West Coast.

CALVIN   A lot of these things start out there, especially in the fast foods area. I can imagine that we will have foil packages to put the hot piece of toast in and take it out to the car.

HARRY   I haven't given this too much thought, but there are a great many kinds of toast, Mary—plain buttered toast, cinnamon toast, raisin . . .

CALVIN   Irish soda bread would make a different toast.

■ ■ ■

POP   Would you serve French toast?

HARRY   I don't think so. That would require eggs and might make it too complicated.

CALVIN   Rye bread makes nice toast, with or without caraway seeds . . .

HARRY   And when it's a couple of days old, we can make croutons out of it.

MARY   The bread will have to be sliced uniformly . . .

(*Telephone rings*)

HARRY   Answer the phone, Pop.

(*Sound: Picks up phone*)

POP   Hello, Pop Beloved, stage doorman.

VOICE   (*On phone*) Is this the Backstayge residence?

POP   Yes, it is, I just happened to pick up the phone. Do you want to speak to Mary or Harry?

VOICE   Yes, I'll speak to either one of them. Tell them that Holiday Beaufort is on the phone.

POP   It's Holiday Beaufort.

HARRY   I better take that. Hello, this is Harry Backstayge. How are you, Holiday?

HOLIDAY   Pretty well, Harry. You know that I'm in the real estate business here in Skunk Haven.

HARRY   Yes, I read something about that. You gave up your theatrical career.

HOLIDAY   That's right. Mr. Nelson came by and said that you people will be looking for a spot to put up your House of Toast building.

HARRY   Yes, that's the next step. Micklebar Nelson told us to look for a location.

■ ■ ■

116

HOLIDAY   I've got just the location. It's a nice spot, and it's close to traffic, and it's . . . er . . . Do you know where the dump is?

(*Theme music, up and under*)

WORD CARR   And so Harry and Mary prepare to go about finding a location for their new House of Toast restaurant. You'll want to be here tomorrow, when we'll hear Holiday Beaufort say . . .

HOLIDAY   Will you have creamed toast, too?

WORD CARR   That's in the next exciting episode of *Mary Backstayge, Noble Wife*. Word Carr speaking.

dining out

Butter it up

by Barbara Rader
Newsday Food Editor

HOUSE OF TOAST

On the Highway, Skunk Haven, L.I.

Assessment: Unusual (mythical) fast-food operation featuring all types of toast; surroundings unusual also; service casual.
Days Open: Seven, for lunch and dinner if you like only toast.
Price Range: Moderate to well done. No credit cards, no bar, but they do serve milk shakes.
How to Find It: 710 on your radio dial (Station WOR), on the *Bob and Ray Show*, Monday through Friday from 3:15 to 7 P.M.

The Backstayges have finally done it—given Long Island its first fast-food toast operation. We have our McDonald's and Burger King, our Hardee's and Mr. Pip's Fish and Chips. And it was inevitable that we get a restaurant devoted only to one item—in this case, toasted bread.

I missed the gala opening the other day, but managed to drop in recently for a sample of some of the goodies offered.

The menu is very spartan, and frankly, it isn't always executed the way it should be. For example, the big

■ ■ ■

118

seller, plain toast, came out too well-done on five occasions and too light on three occasions. Also, the present method of wrapping each piece in aluminum foil has to stop. What's worse than a crisp piece of toast wrapped in foil and getting limper by the minute? I'll tell you what's worse. The Backstayges' version of pumpernickel toast. That sample came out half toasted and half raw. I don't know how they did it (yes, I do, they did it deliberately), but that's what happened. I liked the French toast (made with thick chunks of challah), with its dusting of confectioners' sugar. But the maple syrup served with it was too thin. And where was the beach-plum jelly to go with the unbuttered version? Marmalade is okay, but beachplum is better.

I must talk a bit about the ambience, especially the décor of this newest restaurant. It is, in a word, eclectic. I could say awful, but I happen to like lively colors. So what if one wall is purple, another blue, another orange and another red? So what if the place is shaped like a toaster and that the toasting machine (which, incidentally, spills out 3,000 pieces of toast in one minute) takes up most of the space? So what if there are only five tables and ten chairs in the place? Where else can you get a butter-cinnamon toast on Long Island that's shaped like a fish? (Yes, a fish.) Where else can you get the divided attention of Mary Backstayge—Noble Wife—waiting on you while she giggles in the background with Greg Marlowe, Broadway playwright who is secretly in love with her? Where else can you get a glimpse of Pop Beloved (he runs the malted milk machine, which also takes up a lot of space, but then it also spills out fifty gallons of milkshakes a minute).

I don't usually discuss the personalities of the restaurant staff in my reviews, but when I visited the H of T recently, there were no other customers, although I waited around for about five hours. During that time I was able to talk to Pop Beloved, Calvin Hoogevin, Harry

■ ■ ■

Backstayge, and Mary (when she wasn't giggling) and get to know them rather well. They have put together a rather slick operation, considering that they don't know a thing about the restaurant business (that's okay, there are plenty of people in the restaurant business these days who don't know anything about it either), and I like some of the little touches.

For example, the silverware, including napkin holders, is solid silver and bears the monogram "H of T" in old English script. I fear they'll be ripped off within a short time by souvenir collectors, but while they're there, they add a touch of class. Ditto the Waterford crystal, very posh, but for a toast restaurant? Really.

This is, of course, a singularly risky venture, but with your help and mine, we'll get House of Toast off to a rousing start. Ooops, do I smell something burning?

■ ■ ■

oatmeal
for
thanksgiving

■ ■ ■

BOB   With us right now is a gentleman who's been ab-
sent from our Bob and Ray microphone for some
months—I would dare say almost a year. You may
remember him as Captain Gibbes.

GIBBES   It's no longer than that, it's fifteen to seventeen
months.

BOB   Captain Gibbes, the last time you were here, you
were working in the role of public relations man.

GIBBES   Currently.

■ ■ ■

BOB You're still a public relations man?

GIBBES Yes, I am, Bob.

BOB Doing the same thing?

GIBBES No, no, I'm with the Oatmeal Institute now, Bob. I'm trying to change the average American's approach to Thanksgiving dinner.

BOB Yes, well, you were working on frankfurts for Thanksgiving dinner the last time I talked to you, I think.

GIBBES I dare say it's been so long ago that I worked for the fish people. Right now I'm with the oatmeal people, and I think it's just a matter of public relations, of educating the public.

BOB Educating the public to oatmeal, you mean?

GIBBES That's right. For so long the American people have thought you eat oatmeal only when it's snowing and twelve below zero, and you get to eat that in the morning.

BOB Well, it does give you a great start for the day.

GIBBES But my point is to see if we can promote it for Thanksgiving dinner. There's a million ways you can make it.

BOB Oatmeal for Thanksgiving dinner as against maybe a roast beef?

GIBBES We're working over at the institute now on a kind of form you can put your oatmeal into in a shape of a bird.

BOB Like a mold, you mean.

GIBBES A mold—that's the word I was searching for, Bob. We have one now. It's a turkey.

■ ■ ■

BOB   The mold, you mean?

GIBBES   In the shape of a turkey, you fill it with oatmeal, and our idea is, you serve it as the centerpiece and as the main course.

BOB   Well, this is an aspic mold, isn't it, that you brought and you're gonna put that on the center of the table and try to make people think it's a turkey or what???

GIBBES   No, no, you can't fool—no, no, no, that's not the idea at all. No, Bob, you're pulling my leg.

BOB   You mean you bring it out and say, look at the mold in the shape of a turkey, this is oatmeal?

GIBBES   No, now you say, I think I'll slice the oatmeal and that's it, it's just that it's in the shape, you can have it in the shape of anybody. I mean, I just pick a turkey because you have it Thanksgiving a lot.

BOB   What success have you had with orienting the public or changing the public's conception of Thanksgiving dinner?

GIBBES   I haven't changed the public's conception of oatmeal one iota.

BOB   Well, I think we all like it in its place. I don't know whether your idea of having it as a main course for Thanksgiving dinner would be successful, but all good wishes to you, as we always give you that good wish.

GIBBES   Thank you, Bob, you've said exactly what everybody I've talked to about this has said. They wish me a lot of luck, but they think I'm a nut.

■ ■ ■

webley l. webster:
wisdom
of the
ages

...

(Theme music, in and under)

WEBSTER   Hello, this is Webley L. Webster welcoming you to educational *Wisdom of the Ages*. We have with us a panel of distinguished scholars who are going to use their wisdom, their sapiens and profunditers to give you, the listeners, something to ponder over.

First guest on my right is Roland C. Drob, the Dean of Wisdom at the Druckel School of Agriculture.

...

DROB   How do you do?

WEBSTER   Sir, you don't have to smile perpetually. This is radio. And Fiona Flavin, whose current book of poems, *Rhymes on My Hands*, is a glut on the market.

FIONA   (*Interrupting*) It is not a glut on the market. The note says that it was "put" on the market.

WEBSTER   I'm sorry. Our last guest is Stock Vanderhoogen, who used to study Sigmund Freud.

STOCK   No, I used to study Hans Christian Andersen.

WEBSTER   Well, I knew it was one of those foreigners. Panel, it is time to philosophize, and I should like first to look at Stock Vanderhoogen.

STOCK   Who is he looking at?

WEBSTER   Stock Vanderhoogen!

STOCK   Well, I believe it was Confucius who once said, "Water can both sustain and engulf a ship."

FIONA   I think Samuel Johnson said, "Nobody is always wrong. Even a stopped clock is right twice a day."

DROB   I always admired William Shakespeare for saying, "There is small choice in rotten apples."

WEBSTER   I would like to add a point here. The poet George Burns once said, "Water can both sustain and engulf a ship."

STOCK   What insight the poet Shelly Winters had when he said, "Never argue with a doctor, he has inside information."

FIONA   A memorable line from Shakespeare's *As You Like It* was "Laughter greases up the engine of worry, enabling you to slide merrily on your way."

■ ■ ■

DROB   Ginger Rogers, in a moment of inspiration, once said, "Nobody is always wrong. Even a stopped clock is right twice a day."

STOCK   Charles Dickens knew from whence he spoke when he said, "Water can both sustain and engulf a ship."

FIONA   I think it was Ginger Rogers who said, "Water can both sustain and engulf a ship."

DROB   I remember Rudyard Kipling's immortal words, "Nobody is always wrong. Even a stopped clock is right twice a day."

WEBSTER   I have tried to live by the words of Henry Morgan, who said, "Put your money where your mouth is."

DROB   He's a good singer, too.

WEBSTER   I think our time is about up. As you know, this program, *Wisdom of the Ages*, is a copyrighted feature and cannot be broadcast without the express consent of the now-defunct Continental League.

■ ■ ■

cadenza

■ ■ ■

(Western-type instrumental music. Establish and under for)

ANNOUNCER And now Nimblehoff, the greatest name in nonskid bath mats, brings you another thrilling episode of *Cadenza*—the action-packed story of a well-meaning father and his bachelor sons who do the best they can on eight hundred thousand acres of the Old West.

(Theme music up briefly and then fade for)

■ ■ ■

ANNOUNCER   As our scene opens today, Ben Cartwheel, the legendary owner of the vast Braggadocio, is meandering around the ranch house when his eldest boy, Mule, enters.

(*Sound: Footsteps*)

BEN   (*Elderly throughout*) Dadgummit, Mule, what are you doing here when it ain't even sundown yet? You're supposed to be out a-helpin' your brother Chauncy plow the lower two hundred thousand.

MULE   I know, Paw. But it gets hot out there a-pullin' that plow and having Chauncy use the whip on me. He won't even take turns and get hitched up his share of the time.

BEN   Dadgummit, Chauncy ain't supposed to get hitched up and pull. You know you're stronger than any of my other thirteen boys. There ain't a one of them can get more'n a section of land ready for planting 'twixt sunup and sundown but you.

MULE   Well, I reckon that's right enough, Paw. But just think of how much better we could do with the whole spread if we bought ourselves some new-fangled equipment—like maybe a horse.

BEN   A horse! Dadgummit all. Do you think I spent the best years of my life raising fourteen boys just so I could have the farm chores handled by a horse?

MULE   Well, he wouldn't be a-doin' all the chores, Paw. I mean, look at old Crummet Stillwell down the road. He went and got a horse, but there's still plenty of chores for Crummet to do hisself.

BEN   Dadgummit all. You can't make no comparison 'twixt the Braggadocio and Crummet's place. He farms the rest of Nevada and most of Utah with nobody to help him but Nellie Sue. And they're

■ ■ ■

both past ninety. Now, you got some other reason for a-wantin' me to throw good money away on a horse, ain'tcha?

MULE   Well, I sorta do, Paw. I'm a-fixin' to get married.

BEN   Great balls of fire! Ain't you got no pride at all in family tradition? Us Cartwheels have all been bachelors for generations.

MULE   Well, you wasn't always a bachelor, Paw.

BEN   Dadgummit. I'm a widower. Ain't that good enough for you?

MULE   Well, sure it is, Paw. I want to be one of them too, someday. But I can't do it without I get married first. And it ain't like you'd be left all alone. You still got the other thirteen boys.

BEN   And how long do you think they'd stick around once you put the idea of getting married in their fool heads?

MULE   Oh, Paw, the younger ones ain't ready to settle down yet. You're forgetting I'll be sixty-two come spring. And even the next oldest, whatever his name is, can't be more'n fifty-eight.

BEN   Well, he's still starting to notice girls, whatever his name is. And I ain't gonna have you all beginning to scatter and leaving me to buy another horse every time one of you takes off. Us Cartwheels is a family of humans, and I aim to keep it that way.

MULE   Paw, you're a-holdin' back something. You always liked horses better'n us boys and you know it.

BEN   T'ain't so. They eat more and they don't plow as good.

MULE   Paw, you got a secret reason for not wanting any

■ ■ ■

129

of us to marry up. Now supposing you just tell me what it is.

BEN   All right, Mule. You win, boy. There was a telegram a-waitin' for me last time I went to town. Now just you listen good to this: "Agency brass opposes introduction of regular female character in series. Spot check of audience reaction to trial run episodes featuring schoolmarm decidedly negative. Not responsible for option renewal if boys marry and you become father of fourteen horses." Well, that's it, Mule. Now get back to your plowing.

(*Theme music. Establish and fade for*)

ANNOUNCER   And so, once again, the common sense of Ben Cartwheel prevails over his impetuous boys. Join us again soon when the same thing will happen in the next exciting episode of *Cadenza*.

■ ■ ■

spelling bee

■ ■ ■

RAY   Well, Bob, it's that time again, the finals of the annual Bob and Ray Grand National Spelling Bee Contest. Do you happen to have the regional winners here?

BOB   Our three regional semifinalists arrived here in New York last week. I wonder if you will step up to our microphones and identify yourselves. You are . . . ?

BETSY ROSS   I'm Betsy W. Ross from Fredericksburg, Maryland.

■ ■ ■

BOB   You're the winner from the middle Atlantic states?

BETSY ROSS   That's right.

BOB   Russell Plume, are you here?

BENJAMIN FRANKLIN   Russell couldn't be here.

BOB   Well, Russell was the Southern states champion . . . Well, who are you?

FRANKLIN   I'm Benjamin Franklin from Altoona, Pennsylvania, and I'm gonna substitute for him.

BOB   Well, who do you represent?

FRANKLIN   I'll represent the Southern states, if I may.

BOB   And our last contestant from the West Coast . . .

PAUL G. REVERE   Paul G. Revere.

BOB   Paul G. Revere.

REVERE   From Elmont, Utah.

BOB   All right, you two gentlemen and the lady are the regional winners, and as you know, we are going to give you one round of words in the first go-around in our national semifinals. If you answer correctly, you will hear . . .

(*Sound: Tinkle of bell*)

BOB   And if you answer wrong, it's . . .

(*Sound: Buzzer*)

BOB   Now the words will be chosen out of this barrel which has been turned over so that they are all mixed up, and I think we will let our lady go first. Miss Ross, will you pick your first word?

ROSS   All right, here you are.

■ ■ ■

BOB   Your word, Miss Ross, is "Paleolithic."

ROSS   Paleolithic.

BOB   Pertaining to an era in the development of this earth.

ROSS   Capital P–A–L–E–O–L–I–T–H–I . . . M.

   (*Buzzer*)

BOB   No, I'm sorry, the last letter should have been "C," Miss Ross. Better luck next time in the second round. Let's move along with Mr. Plume, or rather Mr. Plume's proxy . . .

FRANKLIN   Franklin.

BOB   Mr. Benjamin Franklin, you will have to reach in and hand me the word.

FRANKLIN   Okay, here you are.

BOB   The word you have chosen from our barrel of words is "Interfenestration," the spacing of windows.

FRANKLIN   Interfenestration . . . I–N–T–E–R–F–E–N–E–S–T–R–A–T–I–O . . . B.

   (*Buzzer*)

BOB   No, I'm sorry, you missed by one letter, Mr. Franklin. The last letter is "N." You'll take your seat next to Miss Ross and our final semifinalist is Mr. Revere of Elmont, Utah. Will you hand me your word?

REVERE   Sure.

BOB   Your word is the interrogative "Who."

ROSS   (*Interrupting*) Now, wait a minute!

BOB   Give him a chance.

■ ■ ■

ROSS   Well, I had a real tough one!

BOB   I'm sorry, but you choose your own words.

REVERE   Who . . . W–H–O.

   (*Tinkle of bell*)

BOB   "Who" is right.

ROSS   What kind of a badger game is this? I had "Paleo-lithic" and he had "interfenestration."

BOB   And so that makes Paul Revere the winner of round one.

ROSS   And this big lunkhead gets "who."

BOB   And we will be back with round two after this commercial.

BOB   Men! Have you looked at your shoelaces lately?

RAY   Everyone else does! Are they dirty, frayed or lacking tips?

BOB   If so, why not stop by John's Shoelace Emporium and get a cheerful free estimate?

RAY   John will personally explain how his unique, one-stop service works. You simply come in, enter one of the little booths numbered one through two. John will remove your laces and wash them in hot sudsy water . . . then pat them dry on a warm Turkish towel.

BOB   Your shoelaces are then hand-ironed by a little old lady. If you need new metal tips, John will attend to that before returning them to you.

RAY   That's John's Shoelace Emporium, in the little brick building with the crooked chimney over be-hind the parking lot next to the five-and-ten.

■ ■ ■

BOB   The price for all this service? Only $5.75!

(*Murmuring of the three contestants in background*)

BOB   Here with our three regional champions, Miss Ross, Mr. Revere and Mr. Franklin, we are ready to go round in our second, deciding go-round in our Grand National Semifinal Spelling Bee. Our contestants are still bickering among themselves about the unfortunate fact that two of them drew hard words and one of them drew an easy word in the first round. Remember, for a right spelling . . .

(*Tinkle of bell*)

BOB   And for a wrong spelling . . .

(*Buzzer*)

BOB   Here we go with our second round, and our lady, Miss Betsy Ross, is first. Will you reach into the barrel?

ROSS   Here you are.

BOB   This time, Miss Ross—and this is the deciding word for you—your word is "propinquity" . . . a nearness.

ROSS   (*Exasperated*) "Propinquity"! How come he got "who" and I get words like that?

BOB   You pick the words yourself, ma'am.

ROSS   (*Angry*) What's it mean?

BOB   It means a nearness.

ROSS   Propinquity . . . P–R–O–P–I–N–G—

(*Buzzer*)

BOB   No, it looks like a "G" the way some people write, but it's wrong the way you spelled it. So I'm afraid

■ ■ ■

135

you're out, Miss Ross, but our congratulations for putting up a good fight.

ROSS   I didn't put up any good fight, I'm just trying to save my skin.

BOB   Let's move to the regional champion from the South, being represented by a proxy, Mr. Benjamin Franklin.

FRANKLIN   I go along with Miss Ross to a degree. It seems like she and I drew the long straws.

BOB   Well, you did get a difficult word as opposed to an easy one for Mr. Revere in the first round. Let's see if you can do any better this time. You have chosen the word "proximity."

ROSS   That's a pretty difficult word, too.

FRANKLIN   Proximity . . . P–R–O–X–I–M–I–T—

(*Buzzer*)

BOB   No, no, you were going to spell it wrong, I could tell.

FRANKLIN   L? B?

BOB   P–R–O–X–I–M–I–T–Y would be your word . . .

ROSS   (*Interrupting*) What do you mean, you thought he was going to spell it wrong? You had that buzzer going before he had two letters out. I don't know what's going on.

BOB   If our West Coast champion, Mr. Paul G. Revere, can spell his word correctly, he remains . . .

REVERE   (*Laughing*) They are some sore losers there.

BOB   (*With a laugh*) That's right, they are, Mr. Revere. You have chosen your word and if you can spell it

■ ■ ■

correctly, that means you are the standard bearer, the champion of our semifinals, and will go on to our final round in New York. The word you have chosen is "far," the opposite of near.

ROSS   (*Interrupting*) Wait a minute, are you related or what?

BOB   Go ahead, Mr. Revere and please, Miss Ross, be polite.

REVERE   Far . . . F–A–R.

(*Tinkle of bell*)

BOB   That is right. I want to congratulate you, and I know that Ray does too. Tell us what you do, Mr. Revere.

REVERE   I own a theater out in Elmont.

BOB   One of the most popular ones in Elmont, I understand.

REVERE   We are certainly looking forward to you two fellows when you come out there.

BOB   We certainly appreciated the booking when we heard from you. Thanks for being in our semifinal spelling bee, and you'll go along to the finals, and I think your luck will be pretty good, Mr. Revere.

■ ■ ■

announcement

■ ■ ■

BOB   We have been asked by the National Parks Association to make the following announcement.

RAY   Will tourists and campers please stop throwing things into the Grand Canyon? The Grand Canyon is *your* canyon. It is the deepest canyon we have.

BOB   But it will cease to be the deepest canyon we have if tourists and campers keep throwing things into it. And now a word from Ranger Horace Liversidge of the Parks Service . . .

■ ■ ■

LIVERSIDGE   Folks, I'm just a grizzled old forest ranger
who's grown gray in the National Parks Service.
The Grand Canyon is my baby . . . I love it like a
son. I've growed up with it. At night I walk the top
of the canyon and look down into it. Can't see
nothin', but I know what's there. A hole. Mile deep
hole. Now, folks, if you keep on throwin' things into
it, pretty soon it's goin' to get all choked up. T'wont
be a mile deep no more. T'wont be a hole no more.
So, folks, don't throw things in the Grand Canyon
no more. This is grizzled old Ranger Horace Liversidge thankin' you from the bottom of his canyon—
heart.

BOB   That was grizzled old Ranger Horace Liversidge
of the National Parks Service. Thank you, Grizzled.

RAY   If *you* want to help in this great campaign to pre-
serve our natural wonders, use the litter cans on
your city's sidewalks, don't throw things in the
Grand Canyon.

(*Music:* "Grand Canyon Suite")

■ ■ ■

state
your case

■ ■ ■

BOB   And now it's time once again for the ever-popular Bob and Ray feature "State Your Case." This is the portion of the show where we invite you, the listening public, to phone in with your opinion on some controversial issue of the day.

RAY   It's your big chance to speak out to the world on public affairs. So call in now. In New York, our number is Quincy 3-1277, and in today's honor city, Port-au-Prince, Haiti, just phone the local office of

■ ■ ■

the secret police with your opinion, and they'll see that you get what's coming to you.

BOB   Excuse me, Ray, but I think you may be advising our listeners to get involved in more than they bargained for there, so what say we just chat with our first local caller who's waiting on the line? To open today's session of "State Your Case," would you give us your name, please?

VOICE   (*On phone*) Yes. My name is Illegal Left Turn Bronson.

BOB   I see, and would you mind telling us how your parents happened to give you a name like that?

BRONSON   Oh, my parents didn't do it. Some typist at the driver's license bureau did. She got in a hurry and put my record of traffic citations in the space where my first name should have gone.

BOB   You mean you changed your name because of a clerical error?

BRONSON   What choice did I have? When people ask for identification it's your driver's license they want to see. And giving a false name can cause a lot more trouble than I got into when I made that illegal left turn.

BOB   Well, it's probably nothing compared to the trouble we'll get into for allowing you to give your opinion. But let's have it anyway.

BRONSON   Well, I think that people who try to pull off a big adhesive bandage real *easy* suffer more than if they'd just yank it off fast.

BOB   Well, that may be. But do you think that's really a controversial opinion?

■ ■ ■

BRONSON   I guess it must be. I sent the idea to the household hints column of at least fifty newspapers and not a one printed it. So I figure they thought it was too hot to handle.

BOB   Well, it could be that the press is controlled by the adhesive tape industry. But please don't call again to tell us that. Now, for today's second call, sir, let's have your name, please.

MALE VOICE   (*On phone*) Yes, my name is Ethel Merman Strunk.

BOB   I see. Well, if your folks wanted to name you after a famous person, wouldn't it have been more appropriate to pick a man?

STRUNK   When I was born, Mom and Dad had only heard Ethel Merman sing on radio, and they thought she was a man.

BOB   I guess that's possible, especially if nobody rushed over to turn down the volume in time. So what's on your mind otherwise?

STRUNK   I don't think they should allow anybody under the age of twelve to be top man in our federal government.

BOB   If you're speaking of the Presidency, I believe the minimum age is thirty-five.

STRUNK   Is that a fact? Well, when I tried to get my boy to eat his grits this morning, he told me he'd just become my new commander in chief.

BOB   Well, you know how children use their imagination.

STRUNK   I just hope that's all it is with Boody. He's already got me packing to take a diplomatic post in Bulgaria. And I just don't want to go.

■ ■ ■

BOB   I'm sure you can get the order rescinded if you handle it right. But in any case, we can't spend any more time on your problem. Now, if we could have the name of our next caller.

VOICE   (*On phone*) I'm Itchy Rainbolt and I live in a packing case that has the label saying "This Side Up" on the bottom.

BOB   That may account for whatever you called up to tell us. But go ahead.

RAINBOLT   It's my opinion that a straight line is the shortest distance between two points.

BOB   Does anybody disagree with you?

RAINBOLT   Yeah, the cab company I work for. They claim the shortest distance between two points is always by way of Yonkers.

BOB   I do hope your passengers at least enjoy the scenery, but in the interim we must hang up and hope our listeners will feel free to call us the next time we open the floodgates on "State Your Case."

■ ■ ■

charley
chipmunk
club

■ ■ ■

(*Theme music*)

BOB   Hey there, boys and girls! Let's all come to order for another meeting of the Charley Chipmunk Club. And now, to read you today's exciting Charley Chipmunk story, here's your old friend, Uncle Edgar.

UNCLE EDGAR   Thank you, Bob—and hello, boys and girls. For our latest story, I want you all to turn to page fourteen of this month's issue of the *Charley Chipmunk Club Magazine*. And there we see—

■ ■ ■

BOB   I sure hope you boys and girls have all remembered to send in your subscriptions to the *Charley Chipmunk Club Magazine*. The high cost of paper may force another price increase at any time. So order now while you can still get twelve big issues for only $8.95 . . . Uncle Edgar.

UNCLE EDGAR   Thank you . . . Now there in the first panel, kids, we can see that Charley Chipmunk is on the phone talking to his little forest friend, Gustav Groundhog. And they're planning a camping trip.

BOB   Needless to say, boys and girls, Charley looked up Gustav Groundhog's phone number in his genuine Charley Chipmunk address book. It has pictures of all the little forest people on the cover—and the inside pages are handsomely indexed in alphabetical order. Yet it costs only $1.98. Now back to Uncle Edgar.

UNCLE EDGAR   Thanks . . . Now in the next panel, there's Charley Chipmunk getting all of his camping equipment together for the big expedition.

BOB   And notice, kids, that he wouldn't think of going without his authentic Charley Chipmunk camping tent. It's fully waterproofed for those rainy nights in the forest—or for sleeping out in your own backyard. But the price is a low, low $39.95. Ask Mommy to pick one up for you at the canvas goods store today . . . Now back to Uncle Edgar.

UNCLE EDGAR   You aren't planning to interrupt the whole story like this, are you?

BOB   Well, I'm sure the boys and girls understand that it's our wonderful commercial sponsors who make it possible for you to be here at all, Uncle Edgar. So why don't you look at it that way, too?

■ ■ ■

UNCLE EDGAR   Well, all right . . . Now in the third panel, boys and girls, we can see Charley Chipmunk and Gustav Groundhog all ready to leave home for their camping trip. And just look at the equipment they've got piled on their trailer.

BOB   It's an authentic Charley Chipmunk haul-it-yourself trailer, gang. Heavy-duty springs to accommodate five-hundred-pound loads. And it comes with your choice of truck or passenger car hitch. The price—a remarkable low $350.00. Now once again —Uncle Edgar.

UNCLE EDGAR   Bob, I just want you to know that I'm not going to allow any more of this. No other show has commercials every few seconds and—

BOB   We don't refer to these as commercials, Uncle Edgar. They're just helpful shopping reminders to the boys and girls—and they blend right in with your story.

UNCLE EDGAR   Well, I don't see that they blend in with my story at all. They're just preventing me from getting it finished.

BOB   Well, I really think it's the time you've spent stopping to complain that's responsible for that. So just get on with it.

UNCLE EDGAR   All right. I'll try . . . Now look what's happening in the next panel, boys and girls. Charley Chipmunk and Gustav Groundhog are out in the woods, cooking their dinner over a big campfire.

BOB   And look at that beautiful unspoiled forest, boys and girls. Wouldn't you like to have a full ten acres of that fine hunting and fishing land for your very own? Well, now you can for only $19,500—full price. Have your daddy drop in to discuss mortgage

■ ■ ■

146

terms with his authorized Charley Chipmunk real
estate agent today.

UNCLE EDGAR Moving right along, kids, we see a great
big bear prowling around Charley and Gustav's
camp in the middle of the night.

BOB Sorry, Uncle Edgar, but our time seems to be up
for today.

UNCLE EDGAR I just knew it! You've cheated the kids
out of hearing the best part of the story.

BOB Be sure to join us for lots more fun at the next
meeting of the Charley Chipmunk Club, boys and
girls.

UNCLE EDGAR I think Ralph Nader would be very interested to find out that we're just not broadcasting
in the public interest around here.

(*Bring in theme music under*)

BOB Don't forget to repeat your Charley Chipmunk
oath before you go sleepy time, kids. And now,
here's Uncle Edgar to say goodbye.

UNCLE EDGAR Goodbye!!!!!

(*Sound: Door slam. Theme music up briefly and then
out*)

■ ■ ■

children's
menu

■ ■ ■

From Bob and Ray: The Two and Only

WAITER   Yes, sir, how many will you be, please?

DINER   Ah, well . . . I'm one.

WAITER   You'll be one. Sit here. I'll get you a menu.

DINER   Thank you. (*Sings to himself*) "One alone . . ."

WAITER   Here you are, sir . . . Anytime you're ready.

DINER   Thank you. Er . . . Do you have a kiddie menu?

WAITER   What's that, sir?

■ ■ ■

DINER   Do you have a kiddie menu?

WAITER   Well, this is our regular menu. We have a children's menu . . .

DINER   Could I look at it, please?

WAITER   Well, why?

DINER   I just don't want to order from this.

WAITER   You mean you want to order from the children's menu?

DINER   Yes. I like children's portions. (And I like to have my meat cut up for me!)

WAITER   But you're an adult. I mean, this is kind of irregular . . .

DINER   Yes, but it's what I like to eat. Could I have—

WAITER   Wouldn't you feel kind of silly ordering from it?

DINER   Yes, but I wish you wouldn't make so much of it. People are looking.

WAITER   Well, I'll have to ask the manager. I don't know whether we can let you order from that or not . . . (*Starts to leave*) Wait a minute . . .

DINER   (*Starts to sing "One Alone" again*)

WAITER   (*Returns*) All right. Here you are. Manager says it's okay. (*Hands diner a large, rabbit-shaped menu*)

DINER   Ah . . . oh boy, let me see here. Ah! Humpty Dumpty Egg Salad . . . Little Miss Muffet Curds and Whey Pudding . . . Old Mother Hubbard Boneless Chicken . . .

■ ■ ■

WAITER Don't bend the bunny rabbit menu, sir!

DINER I think that's what I'll have! Turkey Lurkey with Gravy and Cat and Fiddle Mashed Squash . . . and . . .

WAITER May I suggest a Silver Bell and Cockleshell Salad, sir?

DINER Okay. Then for dessert . . . I think I'll have . . . Curds and Whey Pudding with a lollipop in it.

WAITER All right.

DINER Oh, and for openers I'll have a Shirley Temple —straight up!

■ ■ ■

food and drink
imitator

■ ■ ■

BOB   It is time for Bob and Ray to chat with the stars,
and today it is with a gentleman, Fentriss Synom,
who was formerly a tree and furniture imitator, I
believe, Fentriss, but I understand you have given
that up and changed your act. Will you tell us a
little about it?

FENTRISS   There was a decreasing demand for furniture
and tree imitating in night clubs. My agent told me
that I should change the act to meet the times.

■ ■ ■

BOB   Did he suggest what you should change to, or did you come up with the idea yourself?

FENTRISS   I came up with the idea myself of changing to food and drink imitating.

BOB   Well, that seems like a little-covered field. I can't think of one food and drink imitator—at least one who became famous at it. I think maybe you have the inside track.

FENTRISS   You would be surprised how an imitation of a cheese soufflé can cause a rush of cheese soufflé orders after my act. The proprietors like it.

BOB   I see, and they suggest things . . . ?

FENTRISS   They want me to work on a Chateaubriand, but I can't get the charcoal part right.

BOB   I am sure everybody would like a sample of what you can do.

FENTRISS   Unfortunately, the best thing I can do is a plate of franks and beans. Not very popular with the proprietors of the fancy restaurants.

BOB   No, not very much profit in it. But go ahead and do it . . . Fentriss is lying down on the floor . . .

FENTRISS   Give me the blue light.

BOB   Give him the blue light, John. He is pulling up the sleeves of his brown jacket. His shirt sleeves are colored like a skinless frankfurter, two of them. He is putting his arms simulating the hot dogs at his sides, and it really resembles a pair of franks on either side of a plate piled high with beans represented by the brown jacket. Wonderful. Fentriss Synom as a plate of franks and beans.

BOB   I wonder if you can give us another of your favorites?

■ ■ ■

FENTRISS   What I would like to do for an encore is a bottle of champagne being opened.

BOB   Is this more difficult than the franks and beans?

FENTRISS   Yes, it is. What I do here is . . . well, you describe it.

BOB   He is standing more or less at attention, feet together . . . Now he is raising his hands . . . and the spring on either side of his neck . . . Now he seems to be trying to pry his head loose . . .

(*Squeaking of bottle cap being pried*)

BOB   . . . as if it was a cork on a champagne bottle. He is making a squeaking sound as he does it . . . still prying his head . . .

(*Sound of bottle of champagne opened and fizzing*)

BOB   Skoal! Pops out and Fentriss ducks his head into his jacket creating the illusion that the cork came off and he spewed a mouthful of water he had been holding. Bravo! Bravo! I bet that gets a good hand.

FENTRISS   Oh, it is a show-stopper. I had the King of Sweden come off his throne to shake my hand after he saw me do that.

BOB   I understand that you do a great spaghetti and meatballs and Southern fried chicken. But we don't have time to see them.

FENTRISS   Sorry.

BOB   Sometime in the future after you have broken the act in a little you can tell us about it, and maybe we will have some more time.

FENTRISS   Thank you very much, Bob and Ray.

BOB   Certainly would like to see that cup of black coffee and two lumps of sugar that you do so well.

■ ■ ■

153

the defenseless

. . .

(*Dramatic theme music. Establish and under for*)

ANNOUNCER   And now, time for another dramatic tale of courtroom justice as attorney Millard Shifton and his son Ferdy put aside their lucrative practice and step forward to defend—*The Defenseless.*

(*Theme music up briefly and then out*)

ANNOUNCER   Accountant Augustus Winesap had been charged with embezzlement after police found him in his office holding ledger books that disclosed a

. . .

shortage of $582,618 in one hand and cash amounting to $582,618 in the other. Circumstantial evidence against Winesap appeared to be mounting until Millard and Ferdy Shifton dumped all of their honest clients and came forth to defend—*The Defenseless.*

(*Sound: Crowd noise and gravel pounding. Establish and then out*)

SHIFTON   Well, Ferdy, the D.A. appears to have overplayed his hand again. Now the moment has come for me to call his bluff. I'm going to put the defendant on the stand and prove he lacks the mental competence to pull off such a gigantic swindle.

FERDY   (*Childlike voice*) Gee, I think you've blown out your tubes, Popsy. While the D.A. was overplaying his hand, he already proved that Winesap committed at least fifteen other crimes more complicated than this one.

SHIFTON   And that's where the prosecutor made his mistake, Ferdy. He's clumsily nailed the defendant on more charges than the indictment listed. Now watch me make a fool of him. (*Raises voice*) Your honor, I call Augustus Winesap to the stand.

VOICE   Augustus Winesap to the stand.

(*Sound: Crowd murmur. Establish and out*)

SHIFTON   Now, Mr. Winesap, you are charged with carrying out one of the most complicated embezzlements in the annals of crime. But isn't it true—in fact—that you are basically a simple-minded man?

WINESAP   Oh, yeah. I was even voted the most simple-minded genius in my class at Harvard.

SHIFTON   Good. In that case, I imagine that $582,618 would seem like a great deal of money to you.

■ ■ ■

WINESAP   Well, without stopping to figure, it would seem like about 29,128 twenties, five tens, a five and three ones.

SHIFTON   But you couldn't possibly know for sure, Mr. Winesap, because I have your educational record before me—and it shows that you never studied differential calculus, theoretical equations or even an introduction to relativity. Correct?

WINESAP   That's right. I never studied those things. I'm just a C.P.A.

SHIFTON   Then how, I wonder, could a man of your limited capabilities possibly keep books that would cover up a half-million-dollar embezzlement?

WINESAP   Well, I guess you'd do it by amortizing the company's long-term debt for two fiscal years instead of one—and then showing plant depreciation on the books as an asset when it should be a liability.

SHIFTON   Your honor, I move for a dismissal of this charge on the grounds that the defendant's evasive answers have confused the jury.

JUDGE   (*Gruff and elderly*) Motion denied. I find the defendant guilty as they come and such a menace to society that I'm putting him away for keeps.

(*Sound: Crowd murmur. Establish and out*)

SHIFTON   Well, Ferdy, you have just observed the innermost workings of a system of justice so intricate that good must forever win out over evil, right must win against might, Georgia Tech must win against the Texas Aggies—

FERDY   Ah, stash it, Popsy. This is the seventy-ninth case in a row you've lost. So many of your clients are in Sing Sing that they're naming the new annex up there after you.

■ ■ ■

SHIFTON   Ferdy, I'm afraid you still have a great deal to learn about the great legal heritage that is ours to uphold. On the delicate scales of justice, small defeats inevitably grow into great gains when one has pledged his life to defending—*The Defenseless*.

(*Theme music. Establish and under for*)

RAY   Be sure to join us again next time when attorneys Millard and Ferdy Shifton will suffer more humiliation in the courtroom as they put aside their lucrative practice to bungle another job of defending—*The Defenseless*.

(*Theme music up briefly and then out*)

■ ■ ■

money-saving tips

■ ■ ■

Another money-saving tip, as I carefully explained to Bob (?), is to wear a conductor's uniform when you board a train. That way you get to ride free and punch people's tickets besides!

BOB Here once again is our Bob and Ray comparison shopper, Mr. Holden Merkley. You told us last time, Holden, that you'd moved from New York to Idaho to save thirty percent on your utility bills. But most of our callers couldn't do that . . . They couldn't commute from there to here . . .

MERKLEY Why not? It only costs me about $575 a week. You see, there's a small airline that gives bargain rates if you help them unload the mailbags at every stop.

■ ■ ■

BOB Holden, how about some money-saving tips on food purchasing?

MERKLEY I'd recommend buying cut-rate bananas with brown spots on them.

BOB The rotten ones, you mean?

MERKLEY They're not too far gone if you eat them quickly. I usually gulp mine down in the supermarket parking lot, and find that I save as much as forty cents a week.

BOB Well, I guess if you—

MERKLEY Another good buy this week is linseed meal. It's down to around ninety-seven dollars a ton, but you have to pick it up at the mill in Minneapolis.

BOB That's good to know.

MERKLEY You can stop in Chicago and buy pork bellies for forty-eight cents a pound in carload lots, which is less than they cost at your neighborhood market . . . by far!

■ ■ ■

emergency
ward

...

(*Dramatic theme music. Establish and under for*)

ANNOUNCER   And now the United States Mint, one of the nation's leading producers of authentic new money, presents another thrilling story from the files of . . . *The Emergency Ward.*

(*Theme music up briefly and then out*)

SNUTTON   Greetings . . . and welcome. I am Doctor Gerhart Snutton, handsome young physician who has not yet established a practice of his own. In-

■ ■ ■

stead, I work in the emergency ward of a big city hospital. The emergency ward is a place where tense drama unfolds twenty-four hours a day. Take the other evening, for example. I was sitting in the office, anxiously scanning the report on my latest medical experiment, when my assistant, Nurse Rudehouse, turned to me and said . . .

RUDEHOUSE (*Falsetto*) Why do you always look so anxious when you scan the reports of your latest medical experiments, Doctor?

SNUTTON Because carrying the burden of mankind's survival is serious business, Nurse Rudehouse. But I think I've made a major breakthrough. Yesterday, I injected germs of the common cold into sixteen charity patients. And would you believe that every one of them is sneezing and sniffling today?

RUDEHOUSE Well, yes, I'd believe it. In fact, I don't see anything very thrilling or surprising about it at all.

SNUTTON Nurse Rudehouse, if you want thrills and surprises, go to Disneyland. Medical science offers nothing but hard work.

(*Sound: Door opens and closes*)

MAN (*Very nasal*) Excuse me. Is this the emergency ward of a big city hospital?

SNUTTON Yes, and I am Doctor Gerhart Snutton, handsome young physician who has not yet established a practice of his own. This charming creature at my side is Nurse Rudehouse.

MAN Pleased to meet you. My name is—

SNUTTON It's very hard to understand you, my good man. I wish you'd look at me when you speak.

MAN I am looking at you, Doc. I just seem to be pointed

■ ■ ■

off some other way because my nose is bent over to one side like this.

SNUTTON   Yes. I see now. And unfortunately, there are many possible causes of your illness that I'll have to check out before I can make a firm diagnosis.

MAN   Well, I know the cause. I had my nose pressed against a store window trying to read a price tag that was turned the other way. And I must have pressed too hard because I felt everything slip out of joint in there.

SNUTTON   I'm afraid that's not a very scientific explanation of what happened.

RUDEHOUSE   Well, it sounds logical enough to me. They're always turning price tags around in store windows so you can't read them.

SNUTTON   Nurse Rudehouse, the mere fact that we've been finding excuses to meet secretly in the intensive care unit doesn't alter our professional relationship. I'll make the decisions here, but not until this man has undergone several days of tests.

RUDEHOUSE   Well, that's silly. His nose is just out of joint.

SNUTTON   Stop jumping to unscientific conclusions. For all we know, his entire face could be starting to slip to one side.

MAN   Hey, while you people are fighting, do you mind if I look at the little babies through this window here?

SNUTTON   Do whatever you like. It'll take a while to fill out your admitting forms anyway . . . Nurse Rudehouse, I'll need a standard 5126 questionnaire and—

(*Sound: Loud metallic boing*)

■ ■ ■

MAN (*Natural voice*) Hey, look! I had my nose pressed up against the glass looking at the babies—and it snapped right back to normal.

SNUTTON Well, that's not too difficult for a doctor to understand. A dislocated nose often corrects itself when you exert pressure in the opposite direction.

MAN Yeah. I can see that now. What do I owe you, Doc?

SNUTTON Well, I hadn't actually begun work on your questionnaire. So I guess a dollar should do it.

MAN Okay. Here you are—and thanks a lot. Goodbye.

(*Sound: footsteps. Then door opens and closes*)

SNUTTON Well, Nurse Rudehouse, my natural gift for healing has saved another helpless soul. So just write down in our case book: "Patient released—cured."

(*Bring theme music in under*)

ANNOUNCER And so another milestone in medicine is reached. Join us again soon when the United States Mint, makers and distributors of money, bring you more exciting drama from the files of . . . *The Emergency Ward*.

(*Theme music up briefly and then out*)

■ ■ ■

light bulb
collector

■ ■ ■

BOB   We have another well-known person with us today. He is very big in hobby circles, and we have asked him to come over. Prentice L. Wilson, will you please have a chair at our microphone? Mr. Wilson collects electric light bulbs from famous places. Could you go into that a little further, Mr. Wilson?

WILSON   (*Very soft-spoken*) You just about covered it.

BOB   Are you still doing this?

WILSON   Well, yes, I still do it.

■ ■ ■

BOB   Mr. Wilson, you claim to have a collection of two hundred and fifty light bulbs taken from such famous places as the White House, the Merchandise Mart in Chicago, and Madison Square Garden.

WILSON   I have those bulbs that you mentioned, but I also have a bulb from a remote telephone booth that you find along the highway.

BOB   What prompted you to start all this?

WILSON   I was a bulb snatcher from way back. I'd take a bulb from the kitchen to bring to the living room. It was a matter of "robbing Peter to pay Paul" as they say.

BOB   And soon after you began taking them from public places. What was the first bulb you snatched outside your home?

WILSON   Police headquarters.

BOB   Were there any repercussions to that incident?

WILSON   No. Do you know the little globe that the sergeant sits behind? The desk where you're booked? Well, the sergeant went out for a minute and I took the globe off and removed the bulb. Then I replaced the globe.

BOB   And he never knew it was gone.

WILSON   I guess not.

BOB   You've brought some of your bulbs with you and I noticed that you have them labeled. Can we look at some of those bulbs?

WILSON   There are not too many different brands, as you know . . . there's your Westinghouse, your G.E., Sylvania. Beyond that you've had it. Now, in recent years, I've branched out to pink lights,

■ ■ ■

yellow lights, those insect bulbs, and your Christmas tree lights . . . your reds, your greens, your yellows . . .

BOB   This one here says it came out of the Holland Tunnel. How did you happen to get that?

(*Crash of light bulb smashing on floor*)

BOB   I'm sorry.

WILSON   Gee whiz. What did the tape on that one say?

BOB   It was the Holland Tunnel. Is that a hard one to get?

WILSON   You bet it was tough. You can only get that when you're stuck in there . . . when the traffic is so busy that they can't watch you. I'll have to wait another year to get one of those.

BOB   I'll try to be more careful with the next one. Let me just reach over (*Effort*) and get that one . . . Oops!

(*Crash of light bulb smashing*)

WILSON   Now, wait a minute, why don't you just leave them in the basket and I can tell you what I have without you having to hold them. They vary in watts, fifty, sixty, seventy-five and one hundred. I have a three-way switch bulb which I got from a hotel lobby in Rochester, New York.

BOB   How many do you have in your entire collection?

WILSON   Well, I can't count the two that you broke, I'd say I have seven hundred fifty-one. I did have seven hundred fifty-three.

BOB   You must have plenty of light in your home with no more bulb-snatching.

■ ■ ■

WILSON Yes, the plain clear type that you can see the stuff on the inside.

BOB Can we see that one? Is that here?

WILSON This is a very old one, made about 1927 . . . Isn't it a nice one?

(Crash of light bulb smashing)

BOB Oops, I must have a little butter on my fingers from the toast I was eating. I'm sorry.

WILSON *(Angry)* Oh, gee whiz. I'm going to get out of here.

BOB I won't pick up any more. Prentice L. Wilson, our hobbyist of the week, appearing before the Bob and Ray microphone.

barry
campbell

■ ■ ■

BOB   The theater season is in full swing here in New York. Last night a new one opened and we thought that you might enjoy meeting the star, Barry Campbell. Incidentally, it closed last night, too. It was called *The Tender T-bone*—is that right, Barry?

BARRY   Yes.

BOB   Where did the title come from, something in Shakespeare or . . .

■ ■ ■

BARRY   No. *The Tender T-bone* . . . it was a story, a
love story. It supposedly takes place in the Chicago
stockyards, it's a period piece.

BOB   I see. Well, now, you had been rehearsing for
about four months on this?

BARRY   Longer than that. You see, we went into rehearsal, oh, I think, last August.

BOB   Right at the top of the heat-wave season.

BARRY   That's right, and we had intensive rehearsals
from August right up until we opened.

BOB   Wasn't this the first show in which you had danced?

BARRY   That's right, and I'm not very graceful.

BOB   I know one of the columnists pointed out that you
stumbled across the stage something in the manner
of a bull in a china shop. I think that's how he
expressed it.

BARRY   Yeah, he has a great way with words, doesn't
he? What actually happened was I tripped over a
small scatter rug that was in one of the scenes there
just inside the foyer of the girl's home.

BOB   Uh-huh. That was the love interest that you played
opposite.

BARRY   That's right. I was supposed to win the girl, but
somehow or other, when the play opened, I just
didn't like her and I couldn't go through with any
of the love stuff.

BOB   Oh, you mean personally you didn't like this girl
that you were supposed to . . .

BARRY   It developed since last August. We were together
so much, and by the time the show opened, I
couldn't stand the sight of her.

■ ■ ■

169

BOB   You just kind of grew to hate her, of course, and by the opening curtain it was obvious.

BARRY   I had to kiss her, and I avoided it.

BOB   Well, that should have thrown the other actors a little bit off their pace.

BARRY   Well, it wasn't so much that . . . it was when I forgot my lines, that threw them off.

BOB   Oh, I was going to get to that, too. The columnists pointed particularly to the fact that there were some twenty or thirty minutes in the second act when nobody said anything. They just stood on the stage looking at each other.

BARRY   That's right. Well, the play, you see, was supposed to let out . . . curtain went up at twenty minutes to nine.

BOB   Usual time, eight-forty.

BARRY   And it was supposed to let out then shortly after eleven. Well, we were still there till after two o'clock. I couldn't remember my lines.

BOB   Well, what were you doing? What did you do to cover up during that thirty minutes?

BARRY   Well, I . . . I sat and . . .

BOB   I mean, how did you get across to the audience that everything was all right, even though there were no lines being spoken?

BARRY   Well, I sat there and I read a newspaper most of the time.

BOB   Well, you were lucky to have a newspaper. The other actors weren't quite as fortunate as that.

BARRY   It was a prop, actually, the newspaper.

■ ■ ■

BOB   Oh, it wasn't yesterday's newspaper.

BARRY   No, it was from last August.

BOB   Well, then, you didn't . . . you couldn't keep up with the news very well.

BARRY   That's right. I'd ad-lib something about, well, the Dodgers dropped another one or something like . . .

BOB   And actually the season hasn't even opened yet.

BARRY   . . . opened yet. The audience was with us, I thought, until two or three of them come up on the stage there, and one went after me, particularly.

BOB   Did the rest of the audience realize that this wasn't part of the show? That the . . .

BARRY   I don't think so . . . They all seemed to be walking around.

BOB   What do you mean? In the audience, they were walking around?

BARRY   That's right. They were walking up and down the aisles, visiting with one another. (*They both break up in laughter*)

BOB   Well, you can laugh at it now. I think that shows that you're a great trouper and can laugh the whole thing off.

BARRY   Well, what else are you going to do? As they say, for a grown man to sit here and cry over a show like that—

BOB   Well, I noticed that you were crying as you came into the studio, but I'm glad we buoyed your spirits a little bit. But anyway, I hope that your next show has a little more success.

■ ■ ■

BARRY   Oh, no more for me.

BOB   Oh, you're quitting?

BARRY   Oh, I've had it. No, I couldn't stand another night like that!

■ ■ ■

the pittmans

. . .

(Nostalgic theme music. Establish and under for)

NARRATOR   *(Deep and slightly Southern)* I don't believe
I shall ever forget that farmhouse in Oklahoma
where my parents and brothers and sisters and
aunts and uncle and grandparents and I all grew up
together. The Great Depression was upon the land.

. . .

But our needs were simple, and my father always brought in an ample harvest of dust to see us through. Thinking back on it all now, one day in particular stands out in my mind. I was in my room upstairs, and went rushing to unlock the door when I heard someone knock.

(*Theme music out. Sound: Many chains rattling and keys turning. Then squeaky door opens*)

JIMMY JOE (*Young boy's voice*) Oh, hi, Ma. Hi, Pa. Please enter my humble lodgings.

PA Well, we certainly intend to, Jimmy Joe. What are you doing in here with the door locked, boy?

JIMMY JOE Oh, I'm just writing down all my innermost thoughts on this two-for-a-nickel scratch pad, Pa. I'm going to be a great writer when I grow up, and it's never too soon to begin my unpublished works.

MA (*Falsetto*) Well, I'm just not sure I approve of this. The money you spend for scratch pads could be putting fried dough on our table.

JIMMY JOE Oh, I'm well aware of how you frown on frivolous luxuries, Ma. But when I become a famous writer, I can make a lot more than these two-for-a-nickel scratch pads cost.

PA The boy could be right about that, Lucretia. I was reading just the other day about a writer named Scott F. Fitzgerald. He owns an automobile and even a tent on the beach in California.

JIMMY JOE That's right. And some day, I'll be making eight or ten dollars a week just like he does. Want to hear some of the stuff I've written down here as my boyish thoughts poured forth?

MA Well, I suppose it can't hurt to listen. Go ahead, son.

■ ■ ■

JIMMY JOE   Well, this is just in rough form. But here's
what I've got so far:

> *A book of verses underneath the bough,*
> *A jug of wine, a loaf of bread and thou*
> *Beside me singing in the wilderness.*
> *Oh, wilderness were paradise enow . . .*

Of course, there'll be more than that to it when I'm
finished.

MA   Well, that's certainly plenty for my taste. Who ever
heard of a twelve-year-old picturing paradise as a
place where he can booze it up with some strange
woman?

JIMMY JOE   Gee, Ma, the only part I thought you'd
hate was that word "enow." I couldn't get anything
else to rhyme. But I'll try harder.

PA   Now, we don't expect you to be perfect, Jimmy Joe.
Personally, I think that paper of yours will do just
fine to plug up that big crack under the window
there. So you put it in place and then get to bed,
boy.

JIMMY JOE   Well, okay . . . Good night, Pa. Good
night, Ma.

MA   Good night, Jimmy Joe. Good night, Roy-Boy.

JIMMY JOE   Good night, Aunt Sadie. Good night,
Cousin Ching-Lo.

PA   *Buenas noches*, Hernando.

OLD MAN   Good night, little canaries. Good night,
Grandma.

MA   Good night, Baby Lucille. Good night, everybody
else.

JIMMY JOE   Good night, Ma.

■ ■ ■

(*Bring in theme music under*)

NARRATOR (*Deep and Southern*) Those dear, sweet voices remain loud and clear in my mind after all these years. My parents are gone, and my brothers and sisters have all moved away . . .

JIMMY JOE Good night, Buck Rogers. Good night, Gene Autry's horse.

NARRATOR Still the pleasant memories of those happy times linger on. For even during the Great Depression, our house was a place of love and caring . . .

JIMMY JOE Good night, stars. Good night, moon.

NARRATOR And wherever I may be for the rest of my days, I shall always carry with me the fond recollection of my wonderful family and the old home where we lived.

(*Theme music up briefly and then out*)

ANNOUNCER This week's episode of *The Pittmans* has been presented by the Kretchford Braid and Tassel Company, makers of fine doodads for your home and fine epaulet fringe for your military uniforms. Next time you think of braid or tassel, rush into your neighborhood store and shout, "Kretchford!" Be sure to join us again soon for another story of tender nostalgia in the lives of . . . *The Pittmans*.

■ ■ ■

public
announcement

■ ■ ■

BOB   We have been asked by the Dean of Women to make the following announcement.

RAY   Girls will not be permitted to eat chunk-style peanut butter sandwiches in the dormitories after nine P.M.

BOB   Smooth cream-styled peanut butter sandwiches may be eaten from nine to ten P.M., but not on crackers.

RAY   This order is due to the fact that Dean Crumbit

■ ■ ■

is a nervous wreck from the consistent crunching which has been going on.

BOB   Any girl disregarding this order will turn in her gym bloomers and go home.

■ ■ ■

the do-it-yourselfer

...

RAY   Now it's time to pick up some more valuable tips
for you home handymen as we pay another of our
regular visits to the basement workshop of Fred
Falvy, the do-it-yourselfer. Fred, I notice that you've
completely covered your workshop walls with adhesive bandages since the last time we were here.

FALVY   Yes. That's the result of a little home project I
undertook a while back with the aid of simple tools.
Water was seeping in through the basement walls.

■ ■ ■

And it occurred to me that those little bits of gauze inside each plastic bandage might absorb a lot of that moisture. So I lined the walls with them, and it's really done the trick.

RAY Well, there's another valuable tip for all the do-it-yourselfers listening in. Those bandages certainly make for a lovely flesh-colored basement.

FALVY Yes, they do. And, of course, putting a coat of clear shellac over the whole thing after you've stuck the bandages up there makes it easy to wipe smudges off the wall with a number two sponge.

RAY Well, that's good to know. But tell me, Fred—isn't it kind of expensive to cover a whole basement wall with those thousands and thousands of adhesive bandages?

FALVY No. Not at all. Every handyman cuts himself with his tools quite a lot, and has to buy bandages for his fingers anyway. So it doesn't really cost a thing to stick the old ones on the wall in neat rows when you're finished with them.

RAY So there you have it, dear friends of the radio audience—just another example of better living by doing it yourself. And Fred, I know the home handymen listening in are anxious to hear the tip that you've chosen to pass along to them this week.

FALVY The do-it-yourself tip I'm passing along this week is a real money saver, Ray. I'm sure you know how popular it's become for every suburban homeowner to put a sign in front of his house with his name on it.

RAY Oh, yes. You mean those nameplates over the gate or attached to a post at the foot of the driveway.

FALVY That's right. Of course, most people have to

■ ■ ■

have those made up special because they're not handy with tools and a paintbrush. But as you can see for yourself, it's quite easy for the do-it-yourselfer to make his own at no cost whatever.

RAY   Well, I notice that what you seem to have there is an ordinary yellow and black traffic sign that says "Slow"—and then you've painted in the letters W–I–N above that.

FALVY   Yes. The wife and I have some very dear friends named Winslow. So I made this up for them as a little housewarming gift. And your listeners can do the same for themselves quite easily. All it takes is a small shovel from your toolbox to dig up the traffic sign. Or sometimes it can be removed with ordinary household tin snips. Then just paint in the letters to complete your name.

RAY   Well, that sounds like a simple enough job requiring a minimum of equipment, Fred. But supposing our listeners aren't all named Winslow?

FALVY   Oh, that's no problem at all. There are dozens of different highway signs available for the taking. And they can be used to form practically any name you can think of. For example, a stop sign is easily converted into a nice house marker for anyone named Stopman or Stopmeyer or Stopnik. Then, too, the lettering can be placed on the other end if your name is Fernstop or Shimmelstop or something of that nature.

RAY   Yes. I can see now where almost any handyman with a little ingenuity could find a sign that would be appropriate for him.

FALVY   Oh, yes. In fact, the chap next door has a nice workshop with tin snips and a shovel and black paint. But he was afraid he couldn't make one of

■ ■ ■

these for his front gate because his name is R. R. Crossinghimer. However, with a little diligence, he managed to locate a sign that could be converted quite easily.

RAY   And so he now has a personalized sign that cost only the few pennies that he had to spend for paint. Right, Fred?

FALVY   That's right. Of course, there was the standard five-hundred-dollar fine involved for stealing a highway marker. But that's not considered part of the actual cost of the do-it-yourself project.

RAY   No. Of course it wouldn't be. So once again, we've seen an example of how to live better by doing it yourself—direct from the workshop of Fred Falvy, the do-it-yourselfer.

■ ■ ■

travelogue

. . .

(*Bright and sprightly music, up and under*)

BOB   This is Maurice Kirkpatrick.

RAY   And this is Patrick Kirkpatrick.

MAURICE KIRKPATRICK   Today through the magic of colored radio, we take you to . . .

PATRICK KIRKPATRICK   Tahiti.

(*Segue to Hawaiian Islands theme and under*)

. . .

MAURICE   Colorful Tahiti, where ancient palm trees swaying in the breeze reflect in the waters of the blue lagoon. Little brown children gather crabs, shrimps, oysters, quahogs, clams, lobsters and tartar sauce along the shore.

PATRICK   Ebullient Tahiti, where joy is king and laughter is queen, and all day long the natives eat crabs, shrimp, oysters, quahogs, clams and lobsters with tartar sauce.

MAURICE   As our boat approaches the shore, we pass a native outrigger. Hello, outrigger!

NATIVE   Hello.

MAURICE   Where have you been?

NATIVE   Out. Rigging.

MAURICE   Just ahead of us, we see a rock sticking out of the water. It is called Plymouth Rock by the natives, after a breed of hens they raise in Tahiti.

PATRICK   We are getting closer to the rock. Closer . . . closer . . .

(*Crunch of boat on rocks*)

PATRICK   Didn't think you could hit it, Maurice?

MAURICE   It's a breed of hens they raise in Tahiti.

PATRICK   And now the natives see us and as they line the shore they say a Tahitian chant of welcome.

(*Natives give a college locomotive cheer*)

MAURICE   And as our boat touches the beach, the natives rush forward and lift the both of us on their shoulders.

(*Sounds of straining and effort by the natives*)

■ ■ ■

PATRICK   And then they throw both of us back in the ocean.

(*Two water splashes*)

PATRICK   This is an old custom.

(*Third water splash*)

PATRICK   Who is that third guy?

MAURICE   I don't know. He came over on the boat with us.

PATRICK   This is an old custom signifying thanks to the sea for bringing us to the island.

MAURICE   And so, happy and dripping, we cross the sands and stand in the welcome shade of the coconut tree.

(*Two coconuts fall on their heads*)

MAURICE   Ouch!

PATRICK   Ouch!

MAURICE   It is fall in Tahiti and the coconuts do.

(*One more coconut falls on a head*)

VOICE   Ouch!

MAURICE   Who got that third one?

PATRICK   That guy who came over on the boat with us.

MAURICE   And as we stand under the coconut tree a line of dancing girls approaches us.

(*Hula music in and under*)

PATRICK   Say, Maurice, the women here don't wear—

MAURICE   This is a native dance called the wingding.

PATRICK   Maurice, the women here they don't wear—

■ ■ ■

MAURICE An ancient native custom.

PATRICK Let me finish, Maurice. The women don't wear any make-up.

MAURICE The women in Tahiti don't wear any make-up. And now the chief approaches.

CHIEF Mongo bongo congo longo.

MAURICE He is inviting us to dinner and we accept. Thank you, chief.

PATRICK Thank you, chief.

THIRD GUY Thank you, chief.

MAURICE Who is that third guy?

PATRICK The guy who came over on the boat with us.

MAURICE And so it is that several hours later we find ourselves seated on the ground, Tahitian fashion.

PATRICK Partaking of a delicious meal spread out on palm leaves.

MAURICE Chief, this is a delicious dinner. What is the main dish?

CHIEF The guy who came over on the boat with you.

(*Music: Sting and out*)

MAURICE And so having changed the eating habits of the island, we leave this tropical paradise and return to the States, full of contentment. Now, this is Maurice Kirkpatrick.

PATRICK And this is Patrick Kirkpatrick. Goodbye.

MAURICE Goodbye.

THIRD GUY Goodbye.

(*Music: Sting, up and out*)

■ ■ ■

bridget hillary
and the
news

■ ■ ■

(*Theme music*)

ANNOUNCER And it's time now for *Bridget Hillary and the News*. The true-to-life dramatic story of a girl radio reporter who dares to tell the truth in her weekly broadcasts . . . As our scene opens today, former Senator Callahan is just entering the rehearsal room of the Amalgamated Broadcasting System.

(*Sound: Door open*)

■ ■ ■

BRIDGET   Oh, Senator Callahan, I didn't know you were in town.

CALLAHAN   Well, I'm just in for a day or so. I wanted to drop by and pay my respects.

(*Sound: Door open*)

DIRECTOR   One minute to air time, Miss Hillary.

(*Sound: Door shut*)

CALLAHAN   I always like to keep a good relationship with the press.

BRIDGET   Well, why aren't you down in Washington, tending to business like you should be?

CALLAHAN   Well, you seem to forget, Miss Hillary, I don't have any business down in Washington any more. I was defeated in the last election.

(*Sound: Door open*)

DIRECTOR   Thirty seconds to air time, Miss Hillary.

(*Sound: Door shut*)

CALLAHAN   I'm just a former Senator now.

BRIDGET   Well, I don't care what you call yourself. The taxpayers can't be expected to put up the money for you to go carousing around the country. I'm going to have to expose you on the air as the common crook you really are.

CALLAHAN   But you don't understand, Miss Hillary. I'm not on the public payroll any more.

(*Sound: Door open*)

DIRECTOR   You're on the air, Miss Hillary.

(*Sound: Door shut*)

■ ■ ■

CALLAHAN   I don't have to account to the taxpayers now. I can come and go as I please.

BRIDGET   Every tinhorn politician gets that idea sooner or later, Senator. And when I get through with you, you'll wish you hadn't taken your public trust so lightly.

CALLAHAN   This is ridiculous. I served honorably in the Senate for twenty-four years.

BRIDGET   Senator, don't make matters worse by telling me how long you've been dipping your hand into the pork barrel.

CALLAHAN   I don't know why I can't get the idea across to you that I'm not in the Senate any more.

(Sound: Door open)

DIRECTOR   Your program's off the air, Miss Hillary. When you didn't show up at the studio, they filled the time with a rebroadcast of the third inning of the second game of last year's World Series.

(Sound: Door shut)

CALLAHAN   You certainly wouldn't try to besmirch my reputation now for no good reason at all.

BRIDGET   You should have thought of your reputation before you started making a travesty of our democratic system. I'm going to have to recommend your impeachment . . . not for my own personal satisfaction, but for the good of the American people.

(Theme music in and under)

ANNOUNCER   And so Bridget undertakes a new crusade —this time to try and impeach former Senator Callahan. Be sure to join us next time when we'll hear

■ ■ ■

189

the chairman of the Senate Investigating Committee say . . .

CHAIRMAN . . . Well, I don't exactly see how we can impeach him. He works for a canning company now.

ANNOUNCER That's in the next exciting episode of *Bridget Hillary and the News*.

(*Music: Up and out*)

■ ■ ■

person-of-the-month club

...

Dolly Madison and Ivan the Terrible

BOB Friends, are you bored stiff because you have to go through life always being the same person?

RAY Haven't you often thought that you could make the grade if you could just start over again as somebody else?

BOB Well, now you can start over again as somebody else—not just once, but many times, thanks to an amazing offer being made by Bob and Ray Enterprises.

■ ■ ■

RAY   Yes, friends. Your dream of assuming a new identity can come true each and every month when you're a member of the Bob and Ray Person-of-the-Month Club.

BOB   It sounds incredible, but it's true, neighbors. Once you're enrolled as a member of the Bob and Ray Person-of-the-Month Club, the postman will bring right to your door every thirty days all of the documents you need to assume a new and fascinating identity.

RAY   You'll get phony credit cards, a bogus driver's license, new laundry marks for your clothes, family photos of people you don't know to put around your house.

BOB   You'll even receive one hundred sheets of stationery complete with envelopes handsomely embossed with somebody else's name. In a matter of minutes, you'll be ready to start writing letters and signing them with a name your friends and loved ones never heard of.

RAY   Now, naturally, we don't expect you to take our word for the many advantages of membership in the Bob and Ray Person-of-the-Month Club. Let us read to you from just a few of the thousands of unsolicited testimonial letters that have come pouring into our lavish New York post office box.

BOB   A gentleman in Ohio writes: "For years, I have wanted to shed my old identity and become the Shah of Iran. Now my dream has come true, thanks to the amazing benefits of your organization."

RAY   From Arizona, a lady writes: "I was thrilled to pieces when I got your July club selection. Imagine a simple housewife like me suddenly becoming Vaughan Monroe."

■ ■ ■

BOB   From Indiana, we received this heartwarming note: "I had virtually given up hope of becoming Theodore Roosevelt after the disastrous failure of the Bull Moose party in 1912. Now you have made my dream of a lifetime a reality, and I'm starting work at once on the Panama Canal."

RAY   Finally, we have this letter from a lady in Oregon: "Life has taken on a new meaning for me since I became Gladys Knight and the Pips. I can never thank you enough." And it's signed "All of Us."

BOB   Yes, friends, a new identity can make you feel like a new person. So why not sign up for membership in the Bob and Ray Person-of-the-Month Club today and take advantage of our special bonus offer.

RAY   If your membership application is postmarked before midnight tonight, you will receive at no additional charge a box of fifty beautiful personalized Christmas cards.

BOB   That's right, neighbors. These are the perfect cards to fit right in with your club selection for next December. Each card bears a photograph of three lovely children you've never seen before frollicking around a Christmas tree.

RAY   That's not *one*, not *two*, but a full three children all handsomely clad in Doctor Dentons and all opening their packages with what appears to be obvious glee on Christmas morning.

BOB   Each card also carries the heartfelt message: "Holiday greetings from our house to yours." And it's signed "Ernie and Florence Watanaby and family."

RAY   You'll want a box of these beautiful greeting cards for your very own. So don't delay. Get that membership application in the mail before midnight tonight.

■ ■ ■

BOB   Just send a check, cash or money order—but no stamps, please—to Bob and Ray, Box 3-2-8-7-6-3-4-5-J-6, New York.

RAY   Or if you wish, you may address us as the new people we're becoming this month through the facilities of the club. That would be Dolly Madison and Ivan the Terrible—Box 3-2-8-7-6-3-4-5-J-6, New York.

■ ■ ■

bob and ray
reunite
the whirleys

∎ ∎ ∎

BOB Are the two people all set in opposite studios, Ray? Miss Whirley and her brother, Mr. Whirley? They haven't seen each other for sixty-seven years. We have flown Miss Whirley here and Mr. Whirley lives here in New York.

RAY He took a bus.

BOB We have them in separate studios and we think that they really will have a big surprise in store for them, thanks to us.

∎ ∎ ∎

RAY Why don't you talk to Miss Whirley, first?

BOB All right, will you bring in Miss Whirley, please?

(*Door opens; slow footsteps*)

BOB Come in, my dear.

RAY (*Roughly*) Step lively, lady, will you?

BOB Ray, she's eighty-seven years old.

RAY I don't care, Bob, we only have . . .

BOB Let's be kind to her.

RAY Step along, c'mon lady.

BOB Sit down, if you will. You are Miss Tabetha Whirley?

TABETHA Ta-Bétha.

BOB Ta-Bétha.

TABETHA A lot of people make that mistake.

BOB And where do you make your home?

TABETHA I live in Bondurant, Wyoming.

BOB That's wonderful country out there. And you are eighty-seven years young, is that right?

TABETHA That's right.

BOB And you were flown here by Bob and Ray. Do you have any idea why you are here in this studio today?

TABETHA I don't have the remotest idea why I am here.

RAY Speak up, lady, please.

BOB She is speaking up, Ray. Do you have anybody you particularly would like to see after a great many years? Someone you used to know?

■ ■ ■

TABETHA   No, I don't suppose . . .

BOB   Anybody in your family, Miss Whirley, that you particularly . . . ?

TABETHA   Let me see (*Musing*) my family . . . no, it's been so long since I saw any of them. I wouldn't know them if I fell over them.

BOB   Do you remember your brother, Frank?

TABETHA   Sure, sure.

BOB   How long is it since you saw him?

TABETHA   Let's see, it must be about seventy years.

BOB   Seventy years? We thought it was only sixty-seven. Well, we have a little surprise for you, Miss Whirley. We like to do this now and then. Will you open that door over there, and bring in our next guest.

(*Door opens; footsteps*)

RAY   (*Briskly*) All right, c'mon, pal, will you step along?

BOB   (*Whispering reverentially*) Now, Mr. Frank Whirley is facing his sister Tabetha for the first time in sixty-seven years. Let's hear what they have to say.

FRANK   What did you want me here for?

BOB   This is your sister Tabetha, Frank.

TABETHA   Hello, Frank.

FRANK   Oh, hello, Tabetha.

BOB   Now, will you go over and sit down in our studio audience, please. Knowing that we have made two people happier . . .

RAY   Why don't you sit together? You're not even in the same row.

■ ■ ■

BOB   You probably will have a lot to talk over, won't you, Miss Whirley?

TABETHA   I suppose, but it's been so long.

BOB   Mr. Whirley, you have anything to say?

FRANK   No, no. You've changed. Where do you live now, Tabetha?

TABETHA   Bondurant, Wyoming.

FRANK   Ah, huh.

BOB   As they exchange anecdotes of days gone by . . .

FRANK   I have to get out of here, I have a dental appointment. Do you mind if I run along?

TABETHA & BOB   No, no. Go ahead.

BOB   And so we have rejoined the Whirleys and we know that we have added a little bit of human kindness.

TABETHA   Is that why you flew me here?

BOB   Why, yes, you can go back anytime now.

TABETHA   Well, I might as well run along home now. There is probably a plane leaving. 'Bye.

BOB   'Bye.

   (*Footsteps*)

RAY   Isn't that heartwarming?

BOB   It certainly is, and it did something to me.

widen
your
horizons

. . .

(Dramatic theme music. Up and then fade for)

BOB And now we welcome you once again to the popular Bob and Ray public service feature—"Widen Your Horizons." This is the segment of the show where we guide you to a fuller, happier life by helping you develop new skills. And today, our vital subject is "How to Use Silverware." To deliver the guest lecture, we have with us Mr. Jason Holgate of the Kalamazoo Tableware Company. And Mr. Hol-

. . .

gate, you were telling me just before we went on the air that very few Americans today really know what to do with a knife and fork.

HOLGATE   That's right. We suspected that the percentage was pretty low when we noticed how many fast-food joints were springing up that only serve pizza and hamburgers and similar things that don't require silverware. But we didn't have solid figures until my firm completed its recent poll. It showed that 12 percent of the adult population can do simple stirring and food pushing with a spoon. But only 4 percent have any idea what to do with a knife and fork.

BOB   Well, then there's certainly a great need for your lecture today. And I see that you've brought a slice of pot roast along to use for demonstration purposes.

HOLGATE   Yes. That's correct. I always use pot roast in my public appearances because it's a food that most people would like to eat. But they can't by just using the hands alone. And that's especially true if it's served with mooshy boiled vegetables on the side.

BOB   Well, suppose you go right ahead and show how easily it can be handled with a knife and fork.

HOLGATE   Using a knife and fork, pot roast can be handled quite easily. First, you'll notice that I grasp the fork in my right hand with the prongs down. That's done to hold the meat firmly in place while I cut it with the knife I'm holding in my left hand.

BOB   Well, the technique certainly looks right. But there seems to be something kind of backwards about the way you're doing the whole thing.

HOLGATE   Well, that's just because I'm left-handed. Most people would grasp the knife in their right hand while they use the fork to hold their meat down with the left.

■ ■ ■

BOB   I see . . . Isn't it kind of unusual for a tableware company to have somebody who's left-handed giving public demonstrations like this?

HOLGATE   You aren't speaking out in favor of job discrimination against a minority group, are you, friend?

BOB   No. Not at all. Please continue.

HOLGATE   Thank you. Now, remembering to brace yourself with the fork prongs well into the meat, you just exert a little downward pressure as you begin sawing back and forth with the knife.

BOB   You could almost say it's the same motion one uses in playing a violin.

HOLGATE   Well, yeah—you could say that. But I don't know what good it would do. Hardly anybody knows how to play a violin either.

BOB   Well, actually, I just said that to stall for time. You seemed to be having quite a bit of trouble cutting the meat.

HOLGATE   Yeah. This is an awfully tough piece they gave me at the plant this morning. I think it's part of the same pot roast that was issued to our senior demonstrator last week for his lecture to the Elks convention. And it's probably been sitting in our storeroom ever since.

BOB   Well, I imagine that would make a pot roast dry out. Why don't you try going with the grain instead of across there?

HOLGATE   Okay. That might help. And I'll also exert even more downward pressure on both the knife and the fork. That's the recommended method for handling tough meat.

■ ■ ■

BOB Mr. Holgate is now standing with his knee on the table to get better leverage. He's also clamping his tongue between his teeth and—

HOLGATE Whoops!

BOB Well, I see the pot roast just slipped off your plate there and flew across the studio, Mr. Holgate.

HOLGATE Yeah. I think it went underneath the bookcase. I'll never get it out from there—and my fork was still stuck in it.

BOB Well, maybe you can come back some other time and try again with better equipment.

HOLGATE Well, there was nothing wrong with the knife and fork. It was just a tough piece of meat. But I guess this does cast a certain reflection on my company and its products.

BOB Yes, I'm sure it does. But thanks for dropping by and giving it all you had . . . Our guest lecturer today has been Mr. Jason Holgate of the Kalamazoo Tableware Company. Be sure to join us—

HOLGATE (*Off mike*) I can see it there under the bookcase, but I just can't reach it.

BOB Well, please let it go. And friends, be sure to join us again soon when you'll have an opportunity to learn another new skill on our next fascinating session of . . . "Widen Your Horizons."

(*Theme music*)

■ ■ ■

rorshack

■ ■ ■

(*Dramatic theme. Establish and under for*)

ANNOUNCER   And now, *Rorshack*—the gripping story
of a big-city cop who wages a tireless struggle to
find crime wherever he looks for it.

(*Theme music up briefly and then out*)

ANNOUNCER   As our scene opens today, Lieutenant Rorshack has just arrived at the site of a liquor store
robbery. Trying to pump information from one of

■ ■ ■

those found in the store, a snarl suddenly crosses his face . . .

RORSHACK Now hear me good, punk. You'd better spill everything you know about this, and you'd better do it fast. I don't care whether you do your talking here or downtown—but you're gonna talk.

PATROLMAN Gee, I don't know why you're yelling at me, Lieutenant. I'm the patrolman who phoned in the report on this.

RORSHACK Skip the alibi. I want facts. What was stolen, probable suspects, the works.

PATROLMAN Well, actually, it was almost too minor to bother with, Lieutenant. Somebody just shoplifted a cheap bottle of New York State wine. It was Château Schenectady 1973. And that wasn't a very good year—even for Schenectady.

RORSHACK I get the picture. The crook using that M.O. has slipped away from me a hundred times. But now, I'm gonna nail him and throw the book at him. (*Calls off*) Steinberg, Lopez, Caruso, come over here on the double.

VOICES On my way, Lieutenant . . . Coming, Lieutenant . . . Consider me there, Lieutenant.

(*Sound: Running footsteps*)

RORSHACK Okay, men. This ugly punk in the blue uniform has spilled everything he knows. And I've got a hunch it may be an inside job. Steinberg, you grill the store owner and see if you can beat a confession out of him. Lopez, get backup units to nail everybody on the streets who's carrying a wine bottle. Caruso, you take the bus stations, airports, rail terminals. The crook hasn't had time to get out of

■ ■ ■

New York—and we're gonna see to it that he never does. Get moving.

VOICES   Right, Lieutenant . . . Gotcha, Lieutenant . . . Glad to help, Lieutenant.

(*Sound: Running footsteps*)

RORSHACK   All right. Now I've just got one thing to say to you, Mister Big-Shot Patrolman. If you're a cop on the take who's in this thing up to his ears, you'd better pray I never get a chance to tear you apart with my bare hands.

PATROLMAN   Gosh, I don't know why you think I'd risk my career for a ninety-eight cent bottle of wine. But maybe I'd better call a lawyer just in case. Can I borrow a dime for the phone, sir?

RORSHACK   Well, I guess even a cop gone rotten has got some rights. Hey! Hold on. A dime's missing from my pocket. I just bought some breath mints to keep myself desirable, and I know the clerk gave me a dime in change. So now we've got ourselves a pickpocket caper, too. (*Calls off*) Steinberg, Lopez, Caruso, move it over here.

VOICES   Coming . . . Roger . . . Feet, do your stuff.

(*Sound: Running footsteps*)

RORSHACK   Okay, now it's not just a heist, it's a crime wave. Steinberg, search every customer in the store. If you find one concealing a dime, kill him. Lopez, put out an A.P.B. for anybody trying to pass a coin with Roosevelt's picture on it. Caruso, you take the bus stations, airports, rail terminals. Nobody goes in or out of this city until I give the word. Now get on it—all of you.

VOICES   Sure thing, Lieutenant . . . Right away, Lieutenant . . . It's as good as done, Lieutenant.

■ ■ ■

(Sound: Running footsteps)

RORSHACK I wonder if breath mints help a headache. I got a real pounder.

PATROLMAN No offense, Lieutenant, but maybe you shouldn't let yourself get so excited over small things.

RORSHACK Small things?! To you, the theft of United States money is a small thing? Listen, dummy, I've been on the force twenty-seven years—and I know what this can lead to. Today, some psychopath will settle for a dime. But then he gets greedy. Before long, he's knocked over every bank and Brinks Express truck in the city. Eight million people are penniless, and one hoodlum's got all the dough. I've seen it happen, but it's not going to happen again, not while I've got an ounce of strength left to fight it. You get me?

PATROLMAN Sure, Lieutenant . . . Incidentally, while you were jumping up and down screaming, a dime fell out of your pants cuff and rolled under the table over there.

RORSHACK Well, you can have it if you want. These days, a dime's not worth crawling around on the floor to pick up.

(Bring in theme music under for)

ANNOUNCER And so, fearlessly, dauntlessly and noisily, the battle-hardened Rorshack wages endless war to stop crimes that still haven't happened. Join us soon for more exciting police drama in the life of . . . Rorshack.

(Music up and out)

■ ■ ■

preston turnbridge,
lighthouse keeper

■ ■ ■

ANNOUNCER We have been asked by the Department of
Navigation, Bureau of Lighthouses, to remind you
that lighthouses are built for the people . . . for you.
We spend a great deal of money to keep up those
lighthouses, and we want you to use them. People
are not using lighthouses enough. When did you
last use a lighthouse? Have you taught your children
to use them? If the answer is no, then you are not
a public-spirited citizen. Now of course, lighthouses
are not situated where the traffic is thickest, but

■ ■ ■

there is a lighthouse within a reasonable distance of your community. Ride out to it, or walk out, and see what fun a lighthouse can be. Listen now to a word from Captain Preston Turnbridge, grizzled veteran lighthouse keeper of forty-six years service, who has a word to say about lighthouses:

TURNBRIDGE   I have a word to say about lighthouses. I've been keeping lighthouse for nigh onto forty-seven years, and I'm pretty grizzled. They's somethin' about a lighthouse that tugs at yer heartstrings . . . You get pretty wound up walkin' up the circular staircase inside a lighthouse . . . but then again, you get unwound walking down. We got an awful lot of good lighthouses in this country. Use 'em as much as you can, won't ya? Grizzled veterans like me'll appreciate it. Avast, now, matey, I'm castin' off . . .

ANNOUNCER   Thank you, Captain Turnbridge. I suppose you're headed back for your lighthouse now?

TURNBRIDGE   NOPE. This is my day off. I'm goin' out and get grizzled!

BOB   Well, that's it for today, folks.

RAY   We hope you enjoyed yourself. We sure did.

BOB   Sure did.

RAY   So this is Ray Goulding, reminding you to write if you get work . . .

BOB   . . . And Bob Elliott reminding you to hang by your thumbs . . . Wait a minute, we've got another bulletin here . . .

■ ■ ■

bulletin

...

This is a superseding additional supplementary bulletin from the Office of Fluctuation Control, Bureau of Edible Condiments; Soluble, Insoluble, and Indigestible Fats and Glutinous Derivatives, Washington, D.C. Correction of correction to correction of Directive 943456201: Please note that said directive, reading chopped hogmeat, formerly reading ground hogmeat, formerly reading groundhog meat . . . should now read sausage.

About the Authors

...

Thomas B. Allen

For twenty-nine years, in radio, television, movies and the theater, BOB ELLIOTT and RAY GOULDING have practiced their unique brand of parody, surrealism, and genial satire on America, and America has loved it. They first met at WHDH, Boston, in 1946, where they were both staff announcers, and immediately discovered they were on the same wavelength. Proceeding to NBC, New York, in 1951, they quickly convulsed the rest of the country as well, and they have been present on the airwaves, in one form or another, ever since. They can currently be heard across the country in their syndicated series, *Mary Backstayge, Noble Wife*.

Bob and Ray's achievements also include a hit Broadway show, *Bob and Ray: The Two and Only*, dubbed "one of the zaniest shows to hit town in many a season" by *The New York Times*; many award-winning commercials, including those starring the famous Piels brothers, Bert and Harry; and the movie *Cold Turkey*, in which they played, successively, Walter Cronkite, David Brinkley, and Arthur Godfrey.

Bob Elliott lives in New York City; Ray Goulding on Long Island, New York.